Meet the Kindergartner . . .

If you teach kindergartners in Sunday School or Children's Church, or even if you just have them around the house, Dr. Ruth Beechick's TEACHING KINDERGARTNERS will be an invaluable tool for you.

Written with the same care and insight as the highly-acclaimed TEACHING PRESCHOOLERS (also by Ruth Beechick), TEACHING KINDERGARTNERS will help you:
- Understand the kindergarten-age child's unique frame of reference.
- Learn the most effective ways to teach him biblical truths.
- Create fascinating lesson times which are exciting to pupil and teacher alike.

TEACHING KINDERGARTNERS . . .
another helpful guide from the
Accent Teacher Training Series.

Teaching Kindergartners

Ruth Beechick

ACCENT BOOKS
Denver, Colorado

MEMBER OF
EVANGELICAL CHRISTIAN
PUBLISHERS ASSOCIATION

ACCENT BOOKS
A division of Accent-B/P Publications, Inc.
12100 W. Sixth Avenue
P.O. Box 15337
Denver, Colorado 80215

Library of Congress Catalog Card Number: 79-53295

ISBN 0-89636 038-5

Contents

1. Meet the Kindergartner   7
2. Bible Learning   27
3. About Stories   47
4. More About Stories   69
5. Teaching with Art   85
6. Music and Rhymes   107
7. Movement and Games   141
8. Classroom and Lesson Materials   157
    Appendix   179

Unless otherwise indicated, all the examples in this book are taken from the following sources: Songs from *Songs for Young Children*, rhymes from *Rhymes to Say and Do*, games from *Bible Learning Games for Preschoolers*, stories from kindergarten courses of Accent-On-Life Bible curriculum, all published by Accent-B/P Publications and used with permission.

1 Meet the Kindergartner

- *A Classroom Visit*
- *Uniqueness*
- *Physical Characteristics*
- *Mental Characteristics*
- *Social-Emotional Characteristics*

A Classroom Visit

Let's walk into a large kindergarten classroom and see what is going on. At first glance it seems that children are everywhere and things are a mess. Near the door are children mixed among some giant pillows, looking at books. Some children are nestled quietly on pillows and others are crawling around. As you watch a moment you see the crawlers are busy exchanging books. A child returns a book to the rack and takes another from the rack. He looks at it for a moment or two and then he is ready for a new book. Meanwhile the "nestlers" stay put; they spend a long time looking at each page.

The noisiest part of the room is a far corner where your view is blocked off by a barrier. You walk around the barrier and see a large block structure. Children are in it, on its walls, around it, carrying blocks, arguing about where blocks should go.

The children are so busy they take no notice of you. The teacher explains, "They've been learning about Bible families, and this is a Bible house they're making. I decided to bring in the large blocks for this. I don't always keep those in the room because when the large blocks are here the children never use the small ones and I really like the things they do with small blocks, too."

You turn from the block area and sit down with some children at a table. A little girl hands you a roll of masking tape. "Will you tear off a piece of tape for me?" she asks.

You hesitate a moment, trying to decide whether you should do it for her or encourage her to try harder herself. You hit on a compromise. "Okay," you say. "Watch how I put my thumb and finger of this hand close to the thumb and finger of this hand. It tears easy when my fingers are close."

The children at the table are busy making houses from tagboard and each child has his own way of working. Kent says, "I need six," and he proceeds to trace around the cardboard square pattern six times and cut his six squares. Then he lays the four walls around the four sides of his floor, and he tapes these as they lie flat. Next he folds up the four walls and does some more taping. And last of all he tapes on the roof. Kent seems to see the house in his mind and he works systematically and efficiently to build it.

"Do you want to cut a door? Or paint one?" the teacher asks when she comes to look at Kent's house.

"No," he answers. "I'm done."

Carrie cuts one square and handles it, turning it different directions, looking at the underside. At last she reaches for the pattern, traces it, and cuts another square. She stands up the second square and tapes it as a wall to her floor. But when she lets go, the wall falls flat. She ponders this for a time. Eventually she cuts a third square. She folds her first wall to a standing position; then she can hold her second wall in place, but she has to let the whole structure fall apart in order to get a piece of tape. She is not frustrated at this. You sense it would be an intrusion into her thinking if you offered help to make the process go more smoothly. Stumblingly, one piece at a time, Carrie's house gets built too.

Jesse has a special problem. He accidentally picked up some scrap pieces that were not squares, and he now has a floor and four walls of a rectangular house and he's trying to figure out how to fit a roof on it. He turns it upside down, thinking he might trace the roof space, but his two end walls are shorter so he can't trace. The teacher happens by and Jesse says, "I need a piece for the roof."

"Do you think what's down here (*floor*) will also fit up here?" asks the teacher.

"Oh yeah," says Jesse, and he begins tracing around the floor of the house. Later when his roof is in place he enjoys the windows that are left in his two short end walls.

He looks through the windows at you. "See my windows?" he says.

You look back through the windows at him. "Nice windows," you remark.

A lot of thinking and problem solving has happened at the table. Rosie held a triangular piece above her house and decided it looked good, so she taped on the gable, and another one opposite it. Bob was taping on his last square when he suddenly saw something in the yawning opening. If he folded the wall upward he had merely a closed-up house, but if he left the flap open it became a ramp into the wide-open garage.

"Mine's a garage," he said, holding it up for his teacher to admire.

"You don't want to make a house?"

"No. It's a garage."

"What will you put in it?"

"Oh, a truck and a car and my tricycle and things." Bob was looking inside as he spoke and his mind's eye seemed to be placing each item until the garage was full.

Marie was tracing around the pattern as it sat in the middle of her sheet of tagboard. The teacher said, "May I make a suggestion? If you want to make a corner you can use this corner that's already here." She moved the pattern to a corner of the tagboard and Marie saw the wisdom of that. It was the first time you saw the teacher change a child's way of working.

You look up from the table once in awhile to see what else is going on in the room. You watch several children and the teacher spread an old sheet on the floor.

"Use lots of paint," the teacher advises, "because cloth soaks it up more than paper."

Each child gets a plastic cup of paint with a brush in it and on their knees they all begin painting from different positions. They make windows, stripes, and other designs. One child says, "I'm going to paint a door."

Another remarks, "We don't need to paint a door. We can make one with an opening." The first child paints his door anyway.

You ask, "What are you going to do with this?"

"It's a house."

"How will you make it stand up?"

"We'll put it over a table."

"Or if we want, we can hang it over something and make a tent. For the tent families. For Abraham's family."

"Look, my paint goes all the way through. We'll see it from the inside."

Everyone lifts up parts of the sheet and examines the underside.

"Yeah. Mine too. It goes through." This boy begins hopping around.

"Be careful," cautions the teacher. "You might knock your paint over."

After a surprisingly short time the sheethouse is

painted. The entire crew helps the teacher carry it to the line and they hang it up for drying.

"When we're in the house we can sing 'Father Abraham,' " the teacher comments.

"Let's sing it now," a child says, and she runs to get her shaker from the shelf of rhythm instruments.

This starts a stampede as the whole sheet crew and some from the table and some from the pillows and other loose children run for their shakers. The names are on them; each child knows the one he made.

"You want to sing it now?"

"Yes," everyone choruses. "This is Father Abraham and this is his flock of sheep. This is his home in a great big tent and this is the way he sleeps."

Even some of the block gang are emerging from their corner now.

"Shh. Make the shakers be real still on the sleep part."

"Let's do it again."

"Okay. We'll do it again. And then we have to start cleaning up."

Cleanup is a messy operation. Children swarm all over the room and the teacher walks around quietly making suggestions and asking specific children to do specific things. Big paper is stacked on the paper shelf, small paper in the scrap box. Cube houses are placed in rows on the house shelf. Scissors, pencils, paints, crayons all find their places. Books get back on the rack. Blocks are stacked neatly—each size arranged separately. Tearing down the house and arranging the blocks in neat stacks is every bit as engrossing as building was in the first place.

"Look at me. I'm carrying four."

"It doesn't fit there. You gotta put it here."

"Whee. Lookit the big pile. Shall I knock it down?"

"No, Jimmy. Teacher, Jimmy's gonna knock our pile down."

Somehow it all gets done and the children gather with their teacher for a quiet time together before dismissal.

Uniqueness

The kindergarten room is never a dull place. Constant movement, childish squabbles and mature planning are in the mix, along with impulsive behavior and timid behavior and every kind in between. When you take time for an in-depth look at the kindergarten classroom you see that each child is unique.

The uniqueness is probably more profound than any of us yet imagine. It starts from birth, or before, and encompasses the total person the child is. His underlying self affects the way he reacts to life, approaches problems, relates to people, or makes decisions. This is not simply "individual differences." When we speak of individual differences we tend to think of deviations from a norm that we describe in our lists of age characteristics. But the concept of uniqueness goes far deeper than that. For the teacher, it means seeing each child as the person he is and seeing his potential and the way he should be directed at any particular time.

Kent and Carrie were obviously at different stages in their construction ability; Kent thought through his project and accomplished it efficiently, while Carrie plodded along, feeling one step at a time. Kent may seem to be the more mature child, but in age he was younger. Mental maturity and physical maturity are two aspects we could consider in studying these children, but that is only a beginning. Kent seems to be high in the ability to conceptualize the cube (a mental ability called "figural relations"), and the ability of convergent thinking—that is, the ability to take all the scattered elements of his problem, select the ones needed, and converge them into a solution.

Carrie, with time and experience, will get better at

this, but she may never be as efficient as Kent. If we could watch Carrie more, and test her on various tasks, we may see that she does better on semantic tasks than on figural ones, and we may see that she is better at divergent thinking or memory or some other mental operation, instead of convergent thinking. Carrie, also, may be a child who makes her inner visualizations better by haptic means—by handling and positioning—than by simply seeing.

Besides these mental differences between the two children there could well be differences in their emotional approach to the house-building task. One could be motivated by the joy of setting out to accomplish something he is confident he can do. The other may be motivated by something far different. And this did seem to be the case with Carrie.

Carrie had been hospitalized for some months and then had come home to find her own mother gone, and a new mother and sister in the family. From this time she scarcely spoke for several months and regressed in many areas of her development. When we observed Carrie building a house it was one of her first efforts after the trauma to manipulate the world about her. We watched the outward working of her hands—the halting, inefficient organization of the task. What we couldn't see, but could only sense, was the power of a personality reaching out, meeting reality, taking hold of life once again.

Each child brings to any classroom task his own unique self. He grows through the task in ways we may be unaware of—ways we may never have thought to put into our lesson aims. We need to keep such uniqueness in mind, even as we study some of the characteristics of the kindergarten age group. These characteristics should not be thought of as descriptions of any one child—even an "average" child. They are, instead, generalizations— things we can say are found normally in groups of children, but not necessarily in all children in the group.

Physical Characteristics

In a two-year kindergarten, children are four years old or within a few weeks of being four when they enter in the fall of their first year. By fall of the second year they have become five. And by the time they leave kindergarten for first grade they are six. So the kindergarten ages discussed in this book include fours, fives, and younger sixes.

In his physical growth the kindergartner has reached a time of great self-confidence. His motor coordination and small muscle development are advanced enough that he can handle scissors, as well as paint brushes, pencils, crayons, and paste brushes—the ordinary tools of kindergarten handwork. He also can manage the buttons and other simple fastenings on his clothes. He may still be learning to tie his shoes, but most problems of dressing and caring for himself are now within his reach.

He can run, jump and climb. He probably will learn during kindergarten years how to hop and skip. His abilities enable him to carry out his purposes to his own satisfaction. Only if adults point out his deficiencies or bungling will he come to feel he is a failure. Otherwise he grows confidently, gaining new skills all the time.

In his preschool years the child practiced new skills simply for their own sake—for the joy and challenge of doing them. But now in the kindergarten years the child uses his skills for a purpose. The preschool child tries to drive nails simply to drive nails—for the fun of it—but the kindergarten child drives nails to build something. The skill now is a means, not an end.

The kindergarten child can usually speak clearly, and he can sing. Many children will not always be on the right tones but most will sing to their own satisfaction.

The child is likely to grow about six inches during his

kindergarten years, and gain about ten pounds. His handedness will be established during this period.

The kindergartner needs plenty of opportunity for vigorous physical activity, though not necessarily in your class time with him if that is only a brief period once a week. He explores and learns by being actively involved with things, although he is increasing in his ability to learn through language.

Mental Characteristics

The use of spoken language is the major characteristic of the kindergarten child. Until this age, the child has used language largely for its own sake—for the fun of saying the words. But now language is becoming a tool. His word-play continues, however, and rhyming, rhythm, repetition and other word fun still have a useful place in teaching. Grammar is quite well mastered, although exceptions to the rules are not. The child is likely to say "I comed" or "He throwed it," revealing his knowledge of the *ed* ending for past tense. His new skill in language is used increasingly for social purposes. He can ask for information, learn to settle his disputes with words, plan with others, make up stories, and accomplish many other purposes with his speaking ability. He is extremely interested in new words but he often may misuse them because he does not understand their meanings.

Piaget, a Swiss scientist who spent a lifetime studying children's thinking, has given us most of the terms which are now used to describe the child's thought. Two important words that describe the kindergarten age are *preoperational* and *egocentric*. Preoperational tells what the child cannot yet do; he cannot perform mental operations. And egocentric tells the view from which he sees everything—his own.

These can be illustrated by Piaget's experiment where he places a boy and a girl doll side by side on a string. The experimenter and the child face each other, with the dolls between. Then a barrier is placed in front of the dolls, screening the child's view. The experimenter asks which doll will come out first if he pulls the string to the right. (The boy doll.) The child answers and then the doll is moved out and he can see whether he was correct. The question is repeated more times and the same procedure followed. Sooner or later the child of kindergarten age predicts that the girl doll will come out first. "Why?" the experimenter asks. "Because it's her turn. It isn't fair."

The child answers from his own egocentric viewpoint or feeling. He does not perform the mental operations needed to work out in his head what actually happens behind the screen. Thus, his thinking is described as preoperational.

The child and the experimenter can try another game. The child is asked to drop a bead into a tall, narrow glass, and the experimenter at the same time drops a bead into a shallow dish. They continue dropping in beads together until the glass is almost full. Then the experimenter asks, "Who has more beads, or do we have the same number?" The child is likely to answer that he has more, since his are higher. But he may answer that the experimenter has more, since his spread out over more space. In either case he answers from the way things look to him. He cannot mentally figure out that they dropped in beads at the same time so they must have the same amount. In other words, he cannot perform the mental operations needed to solve the problem, so he is said to be in the preoperational stage of development.

In problems such as this the child relies on what he sees. This is a major characteristic of the child mind. And in most cases, the child sees things only from his own viewpoint; he is not yet very aware that there are other viewpoints. This is called egocentrism.

Some kindergarten children can solve problems by seeing mental images of them, for instance this bead problem. A red, yellow, and blue bead are strung on a wire and then placed inside a tube. The child and experimenter review that the red is on the left and the blue on the right. Then the tube is given one-half a rotation, a full rotation, and so forth, and each time the child is asked the position of the beads. The younger preoperational child will be thoroughly confused, since he cannot see the beads. An older preoperational child may be able to answer as long as he can image the beads in his head. This is an advancement, but it still is not logic as we know it. Logic might say that red is on the left after all even numbered turns and on the right after odd numbered turns.

A child who could perform this kind of logic, or mental operation, is said to be in the operational stage of thinking. At first, of course, the child will perform mental operations only on concrete objects and not on abstractions. So this is the concrete operational stage, and it usually appears somewhere around age seven. Since children develop at different rates, some kindergarten children will be entering the concrete operational stage, but for the most part, kindergartners can be thought of as preoperational.

When speaking of stages, we must not think of them as steps or platforms with definite, sudden spurts between. Some writers with a faulty understanding of Piagetian theory have tended to promote this view. Also some readers, hearing it for the first time, tend to think of stages too concretely.

A good parallel to the idea of mental stages is our use of terms to refer to physical stages of growth. We speak of the toddler, the child, the adolescent, the young adult and so forth. When, exactly, does a child become an adolescent? The problem we have gives rise to new terms—the pre-adolescent and the early adolescent. We can understand that a person might be adolescent in some attributes and quite adult in others. The lines between all these "stages" are fuzzy and there is much overlapping, yet the terms are useful to us. We need them in order to talk about physical and social development.

The situation is very similar in talking about mental stages. At kindergarten level it is especially crucial to understand this, since the ages from five to seven are where most of the overlapping is. Children within these ages are not preoperational in every kind of test, but neither are they concrete operational in every test. Whereas children below five are largely preoperational and children above seven are largely in the stage of concrete operations, those in between are in the process of moving from one stage to another.

Consider, for instance, the understanding of number concepts. This does not refer to knowing the numerals and knowing how to count, but it refers to the concepts behind the numbers. Children quite young can easily be taught to count and to recognize and even to write the numerals. But teaching the number concepts is a more difficult matter. Experience and maturation and general thinking ability are all involved and these things cannot be hurried along by a few "number" lessons. But your children's public school teachers will probably be trying to hurry them along, anyway, as will their parents and the Sesame Street program.

You will just have to realize that your children are at all levels in their understanding of number. Many of your Bible stories include numbers. God made the world in six days, the rain came down for forty days, Joseph had eleven brothers, Jesus chose twelve disciples, Jesus was in the grave for three days, and so forth. A good general rule would be to leave out the larger numbers— for instance, the fact that 120 years elapsed between the time God told Noah to build the ark and the time the rain came. Then on the smaller numbers, realize that to some children they are simply words in the counting sequence and to other children they are real amounts that they can conceptualize.

The fact that these are the years of growth in understanding number concepts probably accounts for the fact that work with numbers is especially exciting to children of kindergarten age. There is mental challenge on their own level.

Understanding of time (120 days) and space (Jerusalem down to Jericho) are two more aspects that children have not mastered yet. If you want your stories and lessons to be understood by the majority of your kindergarten children you should make minimum use of space and time concepts. Leave them out when possible. When this is not possible, see to it that the main thrust of the story does not hinge on these meanings.

For instance, in the story of Noah's flood it is an advanced space concept to think of the whole earth and to imagine it all covered with water. So the story should not be built on this aspect. But it is an "event" that the boat began to float, or that everything drowned. It is even an event that water covered the highest mountain and all the earth. Now, the wording of this last may sound the same to us as the wording of the first, but the point is that your children will think of this as an event and will not visualize the kind of space you do.

A couple of story excerpts may show the difference. In the first example human meaning is built up. People and animals are going to die. The water is going to do this. So when the water comes, children can understand it in this context. Things do die in it—but not Noah. In the second example, the wickedness is in "all the earth," men will be destroyed from "the face of the earth" and flood waters covered "the face of the whole earth." The writer seems to be trying to impress the children with the magnitude of it. But the size—the space concepts—are precisely the aspects the children will miss in this story.

TEACHING KINDERGARTNERS

1. . . . God said, "Noah, all these people hurt each other and kill each other. They spoil my world. I will not let them live on my world anymore. I will let the waters come over the land. And the people and the animals and the creeping things and the birds will die. The water will cover every living thing."

   Then God said, "Noah, you will not die in the water. You will be safe from the waters. So listen carefully, Noah . . . ."

   . . . the water got higher and higher. And the water covered every living thing . . . .

2. . . . There was wickedness in all the earth. Everywhere men were disobeying God. So God said, "I am sorry I made man. I will destroy man from the face of the earth."

   But God found one righteous man named Noah. God said to Noah . . . .

   . . . and the flood came over the earth. It was bigger than Lake_____, which you know. It was bigger than all the oceans put together. It covered the face of the whole earth, and every living thing was destroyed, except for Noah and his family and all the animals in the ark . . . .

In this second story there is an attempt to explain a universal flood by starting with something known, which ordinarily is a good procedure, but in this case doesn't work. No verbal gimmick of ours is going to suddenly enlarge children's minds and open them to concepts they are not ready for. A better procedure for us is to de-emphasize such concepts, and build our stories around other meanings. This is not to say we change the truth and teach that the flood was small. You will notice in the first excerpt that the flood was still universal, but this is taught not by the idea of space but by the "event" of covering every living thing.

There are more differences in these excerpts than the emphasis or de-emphasis on space. Notice the differences in concreteness. In the first example, living things will "die in the water"; in the other, God will "destroy" them. In the first example people "hurt each other and kill each other"; in the second, there is "wickedness" and "disobeying God." The more specific wording is clearer to the children. Abstract words such as wickedness, destroy and disobey move the story farther from the children's understanding.

Many teachers and children's writers seem to instinctively gear their stories and teachings to young children's minds. There is an art in communicating with children. But study of children's thinking will enhance such communicative ability—study in books such as this one, more detailed study from the researches themselves, and continual study of the children in your classes.

Social-Emotional Characteristics

The most obvious personality development in the kindergarten child is his social adjustment. Before this age the child has not actually had social life in the full sense of that term. The preschool child's behavior was characterized as parallel, while the kindergarten child's behavior becomes increasingly cooperative.

Planning together is a new skill the children can develop during these years. In the classroom we observed, the children in the block center did some short-term, on-the-spot planning, and they worked together to build their structure. The children working on the sheet house had obviously done some planning before we arrived and they worked purposefully to carry out their plans.

Making plans and completing them is exciting to kindergartners. It is a new insight at this age, and the children need guidance in handling it well. Adults can help children plan for a time span that does not reach too far into the future and for projects that are within the abilities of the children. Children grow immensely when they are allowed to work and play together in this way.

The increasing ability to cooperate is seen also in children's dramatic play. As they play house or store or church, true cooperation increasingly displaces parallelism. Children have an abundance of ideas for their dramatic play, ideas which are more true to life and which make use of information they have learned.

Friends are important to kindergarten children. They like being with friends and doing things with them. A group play situation will hold interest for a long time. By this age children are capable of true sharing. They can show sympathy and empathy toward others especially in cases of physical hurts and obvious sadness. Children often will initiate the taking of turns. A child can recognize that he is able to make others happy or unhappy. He can understand what it means to be part of his family team, and he begins to experience being part of a class team, too. He is easily led to be protective and loving toward younger children. A little praise and reward goes a long way in this kind of learning.

In emotional life, fear plays a prominent role. The child's new learning makes him more aware of dangers, and thus more prone to fear. He needs guidance in this area, to identify his fears without feeling guilty over them, and to face his fears. He can talk about them, analyze them, and gain some insight into the causes. With reassurance from adults he can face situations bravely in spite of his fears.

Fighting occurs more often with boys than with girls. By this age children are learning to carry on their battles with words rather than with hitting or grabbing. The give and take of verbal conflicts helps the children grow socially. Kindergarten teachers can greatly speed up this process by teaching children words to use and helping them acquire verbal skills to use in a conflict.

Besides the fighting, there is other behavior, also, which shows differences between the sexes. It is not popular in our day to admit this; some would like to believe that all the differences are culturally determined and we could get rid of them if we just would. But research continues to show innate differences in babies, even from birth—differences in temperamental predispositions, activity levels, irritability, responsiveness and general mood.

Girls, in general, can hear a wider range of sound frequencies (which helps them hear speech consonants more clearly), and their fine motor systems of vocal cords, palate and tongue develop faster than boys. Thus, girls speak sooner, with greater fluency and grammatical accuracy, and use more words per utterance than boys. They also sing on tune more often than boys. Boys' gross motor skills are superior to girls', and their development in this area may help inhibit early development in fine motor systems. Because of these innate differences girls can learn better by verbal means and can do better at classroom activities involving fine motor skills. Boys, in general, learn better by manipulation and action.

In classrooms geared largely to the skills of girls, the boys are more distractible and disruptive. Many times their behavior is not actually more active than other children, but because it is inappropriate it bothers the teacher, and these children often are labeled "hyperactive." This label is given to boys nine times more often than to girls. We have lately been coming to realize that nothing is wrong with these children, but something is wrong with our classrooms, which have not been planned to accommodate children as they are.

Bret was a boy labeled hyperactive. His kindergarten teacher at Sunday school couldn't handle him and talked the primary teacher into trying him. Since

TEACHING KINDERGARTNERS

Bret could read they thought he might fit into the primary class. But it didn't work out there, either. A new kindergarten teacher took over and planned activities with Bret especially in mind. When she was teaching about Joseph's carpenter shop she brought real tools. Bret energetically sawed cardboard cartons into pieces. He hammered nails. He led the other children in "measuring" everything in the room. "You hold that end right there. Let's see. Seventy-eleven." When teaching about sheep and shepherds the teacher devised games in which a bear tried to catch the sheep, or the sheep followed the shepherd. When there was plenty of activity, Bret could sit still for a time, too. Bret was no longer the troublemaker in the class; he was the leader, and all the children learned more because of his special zest for life.

Sex roles are becoming more differentiated during kindergarten years. Girls show more interest in a new child; boys show more interest in a new toy. Girls more often sing on tune. In preschool both boys and girls played with dolls more or less alike, but by kindergarten age boys more often choose trucks. These are the years of budding masculinity and femininity so men to provide masculine models are needed even more than in the earlier years. If some of the children are from homes where there are no fathers, a church should consider this aspect of its ministry as especially important.

Not only are there sex differences; there are racial differences too. This is also an unpopular thing to say in our society. Some would like to attribute the observed differences to culture. For instance, they theorize that Navajo children are more stoic because as infants they were restricted by the cradle board. But different researchers, working independently of each other, have concluded that it is more likely the other way around. Most Navajo infants calmly accept the board, or even demand it and are restless when off. Since the "environment theory" doesn't hold up, some try the "diet theory," suggesting that the prenatal diets account for such differences. But this theory is blown by the fact that Chinese newborn behavior resembles the Navajo, and the diets of these two groups are quite different, though the groups probably are related genetically.

In classrooms of Chinese children observers have long noticed a lower noise level, less fighting, less intense emotional behavior, and a serenity and air of dignity about the children. Visitors to Communist China often are greatly impressed with Chinese schools and think the communists have learned something about child rearing that we don't know. But those visitors could see the same thing in San Francisco's or Chicago's Chinatowns.

There obviously is a great deal of overlap in abilities and characteristics of all children. Children with different kinds of heredity and different environmental backgrounds have many similarities—perhaps more similarities than differences. Yet differences among children are fundamental. Our job is not to conform them to one another or to mold them into docile classroom bodies that make life easier for us. But our job is to help each unique child as he grows in his uniqueness and fulfills the potential that God has put into him.

READING CHECK

1. Piaget teaches that children learn by spurts as they move from one stage to the next.　　　　　　　　T　F

2. Young children can understand abstractions if they are taught well.　　　　　　　　　　　　　　　　T　F

3. Children might be able to count and write numbers but still have no concept of what the numbers stand for.　T　F

4. Kindergarten children have outgrown the use of nonsense rhymes and rhythmical words.　　　　　T　F

5. Kindergarten children can learn to plan together and carry out their plans.   T F

6. Boys are more active than girls because of innate differences.   T F

7. *Preoperational* means the child relies largely on perceptions for his thinking.   T F

8. *Egocentrism* means the child has a selfish nature.
                                                                   T F

Answers: 1—F, 2—F, 3—T, 4—F, 5—T, 6—T, 7—T, 8—F
(Selfishness implies that a person can see the viewpoint of others, yet chooses his own. An egocentric child has not yet learned to see other viewpoints.)

2 Bible Learning

- *God, Jesus and the Holy Spirit*
- *Right and Wrong*
- *Salvation*
- *Death*
- *Self*
- *Other Bible Concepts*

God, Jesus, and the Holy Spirit

Kindergartners seem to us to understand a great deal about God and Jesus. Since they can talk so well and use the words we teach, we are likely to give them credit for understanding more than they do. But many things they do understand quite well.

Our God is a person and not an abstraction, so this helps us in teaching young children. A person is concrete. A person lives somewhere, does things, says things, loves, gets angry and so forth. Kindergartners can understand a God who is a person. They can learn that God made everything, that He knows everything. He knows about them and watches them and cares for them. They can understand that God is strong and can do anything. God's home is "up there" in Heaven. The children can talk about God being everywhere at once, but they probably don't understand that any more than we do. It usually isn't a problem, though. Since God is smart and can do anything, He can have a magic way of being everywhere at once if He wants to. God was never born or made; He always was. And He will never die.

These children do not yet think of God in terms of

27

attributes like loving, holy, just, eternal, and so forth. They think of Him in terms of what He does. In the Bible stories He sends the people manna, or He tells them not to worship idols. He talks to Moses or He makes the whole world. All the things that God does and says build up bit by bit in the child's mind his concept of God.

The kindergartner can learn that Jesus is different from any other baby who was born. Jesus came from God in Heaven and was born into the world. The children can use terms like God's Son or the God-Man and realize that they denote a special, one-of-a-kind person. They can use the term, Savior, in the same way, but the ideas that Jesus is the Savior of the world or the Savior from sin are quite complex and abstract. To some children who receive Christ at this age, Savior can be the One who comes to live in their hearts, or who takes away their sin, but the full meaning of this word is a long way off.

The stories of Jesus while He lived on earth show the children that Jesus was a good man. He healed people and helped people. He loved children. He could stop a storm. He is powerful and can do anything—just like God. In fact, it is no problem to believe that Jesus is God.

Though children do not fully understand death, they can learn that Jesus died and came to life again and rose up to Heaven. Now He lives in Heaven, but He lives in our hearts, too, if we let Him. And He is everywhere, just like God the Father. Someday Jesus will come back, down through the sky, and will take us to His beautiful Heaven to live with Him.

The fact that Jesus has a specific home—Heaven— but that He also is omnipresent, are not necessarily big problems to the children. At times they will discuss these things and ask how Jesus can be everywhere. An answer like, "He is God and He knows how to do it," will usually satisfy them. A serious-minded child may continue to think about these imponderables, but they are not obstacles to his faith. It is comforting to a child to know that he will understand many things better as he grows older.

We who believe the Holy Spirit is a person have an easier time teaching this concept than others. The Holy Spirit does specific things in Bible stories, too. He came to be with Jesus' friends after Jesus went back to Heaven. He is with us too. We can't see Him but He is there.

Probably the best time to learn about some of these things is kindergarten age. God made children with their concrete way of thinking in the early years. A child who knows of God and Jesus and the Holy Spirit in these early years can grow into a mature understanding in later years, and that early concrete thinking puts down deep roots that die hard. We should worry less about whether the children might misunderstand because they are young, and worry more about whether they will disbelieve later because they did not learn while they were young.

Since teachers have become concerned about teaching children concretely we have seen a strange reversal of this intent: the use of abstract symbols in an attempt to be concrete. An example of this is the use of a circle to teach eternity or the eternal character of God. "See this circle? It has no beginning and no end. That's the way God is. He has no beginning and no end; He is eternal." It would be better to just say that God has no beginning and will have no end. Introducing the circle adds confusion. It is more concrete to explain that God didn't have to be born; He always was living—and that God will never die; He always will be living.

Diagrams are high level abstractions. The more abstracted something is, the farther away it is from the actual idea. In this case, it bothers even some adults that the line meets itself; it does not go on and on as in their idea of eternity. Going round and round, covering the same ground over and over again does not help with this problem. Some more mathematical minds find beauty in the symbol and meaning in what it symbolizes. But kindergarten children are far from this ability to think symbolically and abstractly.

Pictures or objects used in this way are really just dressed up symbols. Attempts have been made to explain the Trinity in terms of the three parts of an apple—seed, pulp, and peel; or of an egg—yolk, white, shell; or the three sections of a finger, or the three sides of a triangle. Most of these miss by seeming to divide up God into three parts. With small children they also miss by requiring abstract, symbolic thinking, which the children cannot yet do.

When school aged children are asked whether such symbols helped them understand when they were little children, they usually answer yes. But when asked to explain what they understood better they respond only in terms of the symbol. "See, my finger has three parts but it is one finger, so God can have the Father, Son, and Holy Spirit and be one God." This simply states what they were taught, but does not explain anything beyond that unless, possibly, it explains that God is in parts. One gets the feeling from such interviews that the children learned the answers their teachers wanted and felt satisfied with that. This dead-end inhibits deeper thinking on the topic.

The Bible is really quite concrete in many of its teachings. It is as though God knew that not only children, but a good many of the rest of us as well, would need to think about Him concretely. God, Jesus, and the Holy Spirit are persons. That is concrete. They do things and say things. That is concrete. At times we even have descriptions of how one appears. Again, concrete. When children have good teaching about God from the Bible, it is easy enough to try to teach the Trinity idea from this background—if you feel it is important to teach the

Trinity at this age. God says He is one God. Simply teach that. Jesus is not another God; He is God. This is another of the things, like eternity, that our minds cannot understand, but God says He is one God.

It is the adults, and not the children, who see a problem with the Trinity. One teacher had her children hold up three fingers of one hand, and then clasp them all in the other hand while holding up one finger on it. They learned $1 + 1 + 1 = 1$. The teacher described this with amazement. The children, she said, could believe so easily. What pure faith they had! One hates to deflate that excitement by explaining that naturally those children will believe what she tells them; they are not old enough to know that $1 + 1 + 1$ should equal 3. Of course, when a mathematician comes along and says that the real way to explain the Trinity is $1 \times 1 \times 1 = 1$, then everyone gives up using the number system with young children.

The Bible is our best help in teaching about God and Jesus and the Holy Spirit.

Right and Wrong

There is much activity currently in the teaching of morality. In the secular world, people try to teach it without any absolute standard such as the Bible provides us. Sometimes the standard comes from the consequences. In other words, children are taught to consider the consequences of their behavior. If there is a choice they should decide which way to act on the basis of the consequences. Should one hit a child to get a toy back, or grab it back, or talk to him? The consequences of the first are that the child would be hurt, and children are supposed (hopefully) to see that that is not as good as the consequences of the last, and they are to make their choice on that basis.

In most such systems the children are supposed to decide their own values—up to a limit. If the above situation was really happening instead of just being discussed,the teacher would step in and say, "I can't let you hurt Johnny," and then proceed to teach the children how to settle their disputes with words. Thus a "value" imposed on children is the physical safety of other children.

Moral educators without the Bible have a constant dilemma. There is no ultimate standard, so no one person should impose his values on another, yet there are times when they feel they should impose a particular standard. These standards, such as not hurting others, usually come from a biblical view of life, but often people do not realize this. Our society is benefiting from the residue of a long Christian heritage.

We have no such dilemma. We can teach from the Bible what is right and what is wrong. In the above situation, the Christian teacher will still want to teach the children the verbal skills to use, since kindergarten children need much help with this. But the Christian teacher has other tools to use, too. She can teach what God says: to be kind to others, to love them, to do to them as we would have them do to us, and so forth.

Children in the concrete stage of thinking need lots of help, incident by incident in their homes and classrooms and stories, to become acquainted with what is right to do and what is wrong to do. They cannot lump many things into a big category labeled "right" or labeled "wrong." That is, they do not generalize; they need to think of specific acts.

Learning what is right is much harder. Teaching what is right is harder, too. Ask any class what is bad to do, and see how many answers they can list. Then ask what is good to do and see what happens. The list may begin, "Don't hit," "Don't lie," and so forth. These answers don't count as things to *do*. If you insist on positive answers instead of negative ones you will usually have a relatively short list, if any at all.

This is a challenge to our teaching. We need to do more teaching about what is good to do—not only the "spiritual" things like coming to Sunday school, praying, and learning the Bible, but other things. We can teach children how to be kind; help them think of kind things to do for others. We can help them plan to obey their parents—in specific things. When Mother says, "Get ready for bed," then how will they obey? Likewise, we can help them think of helpful things to do and kind things to do for others.

From the Bible stories, too, children can learn to see the right things and the wrong things people do. They can begin to learn the word *sin*. Sin is doing the things God does not want you to do, or it is not doing the things God wants you to do.

A young child at first learns right and wrong in relation to the consequences to himself. That is, if he will get punished for something then it is wrong to do. If he is rewarded then it is right.

As he matures he comes to be guided by his personal satisfaction. The punishment-reward orientation of his earlier stage builds toward this new stage. It now is personally satisfying to do what he has been rewarded for in the past. Rewards still help at this stage, but are not needed as constantly. Children also can occasionally be guided by the satisfaction of others. To see someone else be happy is reason enough at times to do what is good.

These two stages, as described above, come from Lawrence Kohlberg's research, and they are where most kindergarten children will be in their understanding of right and wrong. These children are not yet at the conventional level of doing right for reasons beyond themselves—loyalty, group necessity, duty, and so forth.

These early stages are the roots of later learning, and it is extremely important that parents and teachers set these roots properly. The learnings in these early stages come from outside the child—mostly from his parents—and he later internalizes them and they become his own. The insight on internalizing comes not from Kohlberg, but from Bettelheim and many others. At the early ages, then, we need to give children the law and it becomes their schoolmaster to bring them to Christ.

Salvation

The child is a model for us all when it comes to entering the kingdom of God, as we know from Jesus' words, "Whosoever shall not receive the kingdom of God as a little child, he shall not enter therein" (Mark 10:15). God can work in a child's heart. Spiritual matters do not require a high level of cognitive ability or a great deal of knowledge or anything else that grown-ups have that children have not yet attained. Spiritual matters are spiritual.

Some kindergarten children come to Christ in a salvation experience as genuine as those of any other age. But the majority of children are saved at a somewhat later age. Those who are not yet saved can, nevertheless, be growing as God wants them to. We do not need to view them as sinners, living in degradation away from God. Children too young to receive Christ, are also too young to reject Him.

It is God who planned that human children have a longer period of dependency than animals. Human children take much longer to mature than the young of any other species. Humans are higher creatures and have a lot more maturing to do than the lower creatures. When we view this as God's plan, we realize that children must need the years of immaturity, and we should try to learn what God wants us to do with them. We know something about the importance of love, security, discipline, health care, and other needs the child has in these years. And we know that we should be teaching them God's Word.

Important foundations are laid during the years before a child is old enough to receive Christ. A child can learn some of the things God wants people to do, and he can begin doing them. For instance, he can learn that God wants us to love and praise Him, and children can love and praise. Children's praise is the purest praise of all. We don't know the ages of the children who praised Jesus in the temple, but Jesus quoted at that time a verse from Psalms which refers to babes and sucklings. There is nothing in Scripture that would lead us to believe that little children who are not yet of an age to receive Christ, are not pleasing to Him.

The view that little children cannot please God, no doubt, is an interpolation from the truth that man in his natural, sinful state cannot please God, even by his acts of seeming goodness. This view perhaps also comes from a desire to teach children that they are sinners, as preparation for leading them to Christ when the time is right. But the Holy Spirit convicts of sin and woos people to Christ; it doesn't take years and years of drilling into little children that they cannot please God until they have received salvation and new life from Him.

A better preparation for salvation is to teach children to love and obey God. When they are old enough to understand that God wants them to repent of their sins and come to Him for forgiveness, then they will see the need for obeying in this too.

Another matter that teachers have concerned themselves with is the question of just how much theology children need to understand in order to be saved. Some would say, "No one can be saved unless he understands that Christ died for his sins." On the other hand are those who study the child mind who say that young children cannot understand the logic in such a proposition. According to Piagetian theory, which is the dominant view today, the child mind is preoperational, or pre-logical.

To understand that Christ died for our sins takes more logic than may at first appear to us who are so familiar with the truth. First, consider the concept of sin—that all are sinners, that I am a sinner, that sin must be punished with death so I deserve death. Next, comes the idea of substitution—that Christ died in my place, so I don't have to die. These few ideas constitute only a bare minimum of those involved in the statement. Another concept, for instance, is that the death we are saved from is spiritual death, or everlasting separation from God, rather than physical death, and even physical death is a concept children need time to acquire. Still another idea is that Jesus is God's Son, and sinless, and therefore can pay for all sin by His death.

There are many other ideas embodied in the simple statement that "Christ died for our sins." But even staying with a minimum basic selection of ideas we have a chain of the logic which looks like this.

I am a ——————————→ I deserve ——————————→ Christ died
sinner.   therefore   death.   but   for me.

This chain can be extended at the right to include steps of receiving Christ and thus receiving life instead of death. It can be extended at the left to begin with Adam's sin.

The child who says the tall glass contains more beads than the shallow dish is said to answer this way because he focuses only on one feature—height. He is incapable of considering both height and breadth and relating the two ideas to come up with the correct answer. Such a preoperational child is also incapable of relating complex ideas to understand in a formal way the logic of the plan of salvation.

Recent research is shedding some light on the question of why children seem to their teachers and parents at times to be quite advanced in their thinking, yet in tests of formal logic they show low ability. One aspect of this research concerns what might be called "human meaning." This indicates that children may not understand the concept that sin requires a savior, but when a child feels himself to be a sinner the problem takes on a personal, human meaning, and it is no longer logic. It then makes *human sense* to receive Jesus as his Savior from sin.

Salvation is not primarily a cognitive experience. It is accomplished by the Holy Spirit and is a spiritual experience. All of us probably know of people who were saved even at a much later age than kindergarten who understood at the time very little of what happened. One school teacher who was saved as an adult says, "I didn't even know the meaning of sin. I heard about Hell and I knew I should obey God in order to avoid Hell. On a tract someone gave me, the one verse that hit me was about confessing Christ before men. I knew I had to confess Him to someone, and I walked the streets trying to decide where to go, and getting up courage to do it. Finally I went to my grandmother's house and a great burden fell from me as I tried to tell her about it." This lady further explains that she had no understanding at that time of Christ's atoning death, of the need for blood sacrifice for sins, or any of the many things she learned later about salvation.

Kindergarten children come to their parents or teachers and say, "I want to be saved," or "I want to give my heart to Jesus," or whatever terminology they have been taught and are familiar with. At such a time we need to help them make the transaction with God. It is not a time to say in effect, "Are you sure you understand what you are doing? Let me explain that the Bible says we all have sinned . . ." and so forth.

Some children seem to come to Christ when they are convicted about wrongdoing or an ugly attitude and they feel the need of forgiveness. Some children want to be saved, or become part of God's family, so they can go to Heaven when they die. Some children just seem eager to do what they are supposed to do, so when they learn that God wants them to give their hearts to Him they do it. All these are humanly meaningful situations, with the complex interplay of motives, purposes and understandable context.

One family was talking about being saved as they drove home from church. Five-year-old Jeff asked, "Am I saved?"

His mother said, "Well, I don't know. It's something you have to do yourself."

"How do I do it?"

"You pray to Jesus and ask Him to come into your heart and save you."

There was silence in the back seat for a brief time. Then Jeff said, "Okay, I'm saved now."

Some might be concerned about whether Jeff understood that Jesus died for his sins. Others might object that Jeff wasn't instructed to ask forgiveness for his sins. Still others might object to the "come into your heart" phrase. But this writing is many years after the event and it seems certain that Jeff was actually saved at that time.

Many children will ask to be saved several times during their early years. Since we cannot be certain whether any particular decision time, such as Jeff's, is the genuine one, it is best to simply try to help the child each time he asks. The additional times may be because the child is not assured of his salvation or they may be because he was not genuinely saved the first time. Such seeking children will eventually find salvation and assurance. It is best for us not to say, "You don't need to be saved again. You were saved at VBS last year, remember?"

It probably is a mistake for us to take the initiative in

announcing around to family and church that Johnny was saved at such and such a time. Many a child has grown up knowing he was not saved but afraid to make a public profession because everyone in his church thinks he already is saved. This problem, of course, is not insurmountable, but it would be better if we do not create such problems. With young children, as with all ages, it is usually better to let the new Christian do his own announcing. He needs the strengthening that comes from confessing Christ with his own mouth. Little children can be taught to do this, as well as they can be taught to receive Christ.

The question of what terminology to use with young children has been widely discussed. We are advised on all sides not to use the word "heart" because children will think of cutting out the physical heart or of a man squeezing into the heart to live there—both rather frightening thoughts. The advice is sometimes backed up by citing an instance or two where this has happened with children. But for every child who has this experience there are scores who associate heart with love, valentines, and Sunday school talk, instead of with surgery.

It has been suggested that we use the word *life* instead of *heart,* but if the problem with heart is supposed to be that children think of the heart of flesh, what might they think when we ask them to give their lives to Jesus? The phrase "give your life" could possibly conjure up as bloody an image as "give your heart," and one of these days someone may come up with an example of this happening with a child. If there is a problem with one it seems there can be a problem with the other also.

Probably the best approach is to use several different ways to explain salvation. One way will work for one child and another way for another child. One child will be saved by asking God to take him into His family; one will receive God's free gift of eternal life; another will ask

Jesus to come into his heart; still another will declare that he believes on Jesus Christ. These and other phrases that we use are really not critical. We have worried about them, as though a child's salvation depends on the words we use. But when the Holy Spirit is convicting a child of his sin and the child turns to us for help we can use our favorite terminology and it probably will work. If a particular child seems not to understand, we can try explaining what we mean, by using another kind of wording. In conversation with the child it is not too difficult to figure out where any trouble spot might be.

That genuine conversation with the child is probably the key to most of the problems in communication. One kind of problem arises when a teacher leads a child through a set "routine" of receiving Jesus and then assumes the child is saved. Another problem is when a teacher gives a group invitation. Children of kindergarten age too often do not respond as individuals in such a situation; they just do what others in the group do.

Probably the best general formula to use is (1) patient teaching about salvation—many times, many ways—and (2) waiting for individual children to come to you for times of decisions. If your children are from Christian homes, they usually will go to their parents rather than to their teacher, and that is as it should be. You wouldn't want to deprive the parents of the joy of leading their own children to Christ, and you can feel assured that your teaching helps.

If you are the only person who talks to the child about spiritual things, then he may come to you when he wants guidance in being saved. But that is not an everyday occurrence for kindergarten teachers because the large majority of children simply are not ready at this age to be saved. Your teaching is foundational; and actual salvation, in most cases, comes later on.

Death

Several researches, following Piagetian theory, have been made on children's understanding of death, and the usual Piagetian "stages" are described. At first the children can talk of death by describing it. Dead people lie down, without moving, their arms outstretched, and their eyes closed. The position is what makes deadness. These children can make each other "dead" in their play, but they don't stay dead. The irrevocability of death is not yet part of their thinking. There is little "affect" or emotion involved with death. At this stage, Bible stories involving death are not necessarily the violent stories we imagine them to be for children. The children do not understand death well enough for the full impact to hit them. (Television violence, where there are chasing, "roughing up," and other physically violent acts visually portrayed either with or without associated death, is another matter.)

From the "description" stage of understanding, children move on to the "function" stage. In this stage children understand that the body is not working when it is dead. At first they see only obvious dysfunctions—dead people don't move, speak, blink their eyes and so forth. They get hungry but they can't eat because they can't move their hands. They hear, but they can't answer, and so forth. Later, the less obvious dysfunctions are included in the concept of death. A dead person can't hear or smell the flowers, his heart and other insides don't work, he can't dream or think. Some children in this stage begin to understand the universality of death. From meeting it over and over in stories and elsewhere they begin to see that it happens to everyone, and is generally associated with old age, except for violence. This universal idea of death is somewhat incomplete, in that it rests only on the fact that it *does* happen to everyone, but not also on the fact that it *must* happen—the logico-necessity aspect.

The final stage of understanding death is the formal, abstract idea that death is a state. It is death that causes the dysfunction understood in the second stage and the immobility understood in the first stage. Children at this stage can think of heart death, brain death, and so forth. Those with some teaching of an afterlife may say, "He's really not there; it's just his body." These ideas are not fully formed until about age 11, the usual age given for beginning abstract thinking.

The ages from three to six, which include all the kindergarten years, is the period of most rapid development of this concept. By age seven, children hold in some manner most of the components that adults hold in the death concept—components such as irrevocability, universality, dysfunctionality, and others. Under age six there is a great difference in understanding between those children who have had a close experience with death, and those who have not. After age six those differences even out.

The secular researches, of course, do not investigate ideas of life after death, or ideas of Heaven and Hell in relation to death. One Christian-oriented research connected all these topics and found, in general, the same sequence of understanding, with full development reached at about age eleven.

The kindergarten years of rapid development in these understandings are probably ideal years for us to teach our Christian concepts. Since Heaven and Hell can be thought of as concrete places, it is easy to talk about these with kindergartners. Death, as moving from this world into Heaven to live with Jesus, is well within the grasp of children in the second stage of the sequence described above. Some of the associated concepts may be slower in developing, such as the concepts of soul and body being separated, the soul being the real person and the body being only his earthly home, and the eventual resurrection of the body. These and related Christian concepts that we wish to teach can all be presented during the kindergarten years, and the children will grow rapidly in their understanding of them. The time is right for this teaching.

Self

Much concern is spent these days on the matter of developing healthy self-concept in children. The idea behind the concern is commendable; children, and all of us, do need to feel good about ourselves. But the advice given and the lessons written to achieve this aim are not always so wise. The approach of saying repeatedly to the child, "You are special," does not do the job. The approach which says, "You are special and you must learn about your rights," is actually damaging.

This kind of teaching and philosophy is receiving such emphasis today that psychiatrists now have a resurgence of a "disease" called narcissism. Narcissus, in an ancient tale, was so in love with his own reflection in the waters of a spring that he could love no one else. He pined away at the spring until he died. A flower is said to have sprung up at the spot, and we call it the narcissus.

The Bible teaches us to love others, and serve others. In doing this we are serving the Lord. People feel good about themselves when they are doing this—when they are useful and accomplishing something. Children feel good about themselves when they are learning and growing in their abilities. The best way to help children *feel* adequate is to help them *be* adequate.

A healthy concept of self is based on a realistic appraisal. Paul tells us not to think of ourselves more highly than we ought to think, and if anyone thinks himself to be something when he is nothing, he deceives himself. Teachers' praise of children needs to be sincere, based on reality. Children can learn to feel good about their effort, their improvement, their learning, their kind and helpful acts, and their appearance. Overblown, insincere praise probably doesn't deceive most children. But if it does deceive some, it will only succeed in causing them to think more highly of themselves than they ought to think.

A healthy, biblical concept of self gives due credit to God. God has made us what we are, we belong to Him, and we should use our abilities for Him. Kindergarten children can develop the roots of such a lifelong attitude. We can help them desire to use their lives in service for the glory of God, instead of squandering their lives for self.

Most children already have a humble, teachable attitude, and it is easy to show them that this is good. A Bible story about Timothy listening and learning God's Word can be an example to the children. Samuel listened to God. Moses listened to God's words, and he tells the parents to teach them to the children. Children's major job in life is learning. When they see that God wants them to do this, and when they are doing it, then they can feel good about themselves. Children can learn that God made their hands and wants them to do good with them. Children can be thankful for the things they can do with their hands and the things they will learn to do as they get older. They can learn that God gave them eyes; they should choose to look at good and beautiful things and turn away from violent TV programs and other ugly and bad things. They can learn about their ears, feet, mouth, mind, and whole self in a similar manner, learning to make choices even now to use what God has given them.

God is the Creator; the child is the creature. When the child (or anyone) keeps these in proper perspective the result is a healthy self-concept. When the view of self grows too big, and God exists to serve such a special person, there is trouble ahead.

The child gains his self-confidence mostly from his relationships with the important people in his life—parents first, then teachers and others—and not primarily from lessons teaching him to be self-confident. As teacher you need to accept him and treat him with respect. You need to know when to commend him for his efforts and when to spur him to greater effort. You need to point out to him in specifics what he has learned. Your attitude and your relationship with him is your most powerful classroom tool for building a healthy self-concept.

Other Bible Concepts

By kindergarten ages it is becoming easier to teach such things as Heaven, Hell, and angels. All of these can be thought of concretely. Angels are beings who appear in brightness or as men, and who bring messages from God to people in the Bible stories. Heaven and Hell are places where people go after they die. The Bible is a book with God's words; it tells us what God wants us to know. Prayer is talking to God. Worship is singing or saying our praise to God, thinking about Him, and giving to His work. The actual activities that take place in children's worship time is what worship is to the children. Eternal life goes on and on; it is easier to think this than to think of an end when we are no more.

Such major biblical concepts can be thought of concretely, with no real distortion of their meaning, only perhaps an incompleteness of meaning, which will be filled in as the child matures. In some cases the literal, concrete meaning may be closer to the truth than we yet know. For instance, with the Bible use of the word *heart,* we are fond of saying, "That doesn't really mean the muscle heart that pumps blood; it means our mind or our love." But this all may change soon, and science may tell us that indeed the heart does instruct the brain. Doctors John and Beatrice Lacey of Fels Research Institute, Yellow Springs, Ohio have contributed years of rigorous research on problems of interaction between the heart and the brain. They find considerable evidence that the heart plays a central role in affecting behavior. It "talks" to the brain and the brain responds. Learning something by heart, loving or doing with all our hearts, may be more literally true than we now imagine.

At kindergarten age the children will readily believe us if we say that God made the stars; they don't yet know that stars are hard to make. If the bush burns without burning up, there's no problem believing that. We would have more trouble teaching the logical necessity for bushes to be consumed when they burn.

Since so much has been written about thinking in the preoperational and the concrete operational stages, some have feared that we are teaching the Bible too soon. Some feel we should wait until children can understand it at a more mature level, but it would be a tragedy to wait. We can safely let the children think as children, and when they become men they will put away childish things.

READING CHECK

1. Kindergarten children think of God in terms of what He does rather than what He is.   T F

2. Kindergarten children think of Jesus as only a man, since they think in concrete terms.   T F

3. Diagrams are a good way to make abstract ideas concrete.   T F

4. Children can more easily name things they should not do, than things they should do.   T F

5. Death is too morbid a subject for young children. T F

6. The best way to develop healthy self-concept is to have lessons teaching the children that they are special.   T F

7. Kindergarten children can begin learning about many major biblical concepts.   T F

Answers: 1—T, 2—F, 3—F, 4—T, 5—F, 6—F, 7—T

3 About Stories

- *Stories Are Whole*
- *Stories as Art*
- *Stories for Learning*
- *Varieties of Visuals*
- *Participation Stories*

Many children, hearing the story of Joseph, are caught up with the Cinderella aspects of the story. It's a good, happy feeling when everything turns out so well in the end. And this is just the way it was for one little boy some years ago.

Time passed and the boy became a man with boys of his own, and from his father perspective Joseph looked like a spoiled kid. He argued with his Christian wife. "See what these Christians are like? Just arrogant, holier-than-thou types. Joseph's supposed to be such a great man, and look at him."

The wife explained that the Bible doesn't try to make super-people out of its characters. It is entirely truthful and shows faults as well as strengths. And if Joseph was a braggart and a conceited kid then maybe that's why God had to bring trials into his life—to mold his character into something more honorable and usable.

With no one defending Joseph, the man had nothing to argue about. He also had something new to think on. Developing character was something he knew about now; he could see it happening in his own growing boys. Soon after, the man became a Christian.

Stories Are Whole

Psychiatrist Bruno Bettelheim has said of stories that their deepest meaning will be different for each person, and different for the same person at various moments in his life. The experience of the man cited above is an illustration of this. We may try to pull out a few threads of teaching from a story and offer them to our pupils to "meet their needs" or some other purpose known to our adult minds. But the strength of stories is precisely that we are not entirely successful in our purposes. Stories are whole cloth. They accomplish much more than we could plan for in our unravelings of them.

Early foundations of right and wrong, early experience with justice, bravery, kindness, all can come from stories. Sorrow and tragedy can gain a sweet and noble character that lift the view of life above the daily humdrum. None can count the multitudes of people who were inspired to make something of their own lives because of great biographical literature, either in the Bible or out. Bible stories show all life as related to God. Shepherds, kings, nations—God is over all. Children raised on these stories are infused with a God-view that reaches where we teachers may never have thought to reach.

Sometimes the small events that may even escape our notice turn out to be the salient incidents in children's learning. A child may pore over a picture in his Bible story book, lost in thought. He sees Joseph walking out across the landscape. What a stretched-out landscape for a city child; he remembers seeing something like that once, on a vacation. If he walked to that line out there, then another hill is beyond that. If he were Joseph maybe he'd run. What fun to run over a field like that. And when he got over the line he wouldn't get lost; he'd act big like Joseph; his father could depend on him.

Such a child is "identifying" with Joseph and there is no way for us to predict what this might do for the child. He grows a little—right there on the spot. Something happens within him as a human, as he identifies with another human. Some day he may come to write one of the most insightful studies of Joseph ever yet written. But that is only one possibility out of millions. We do not know the other millions of directions the child's new growth may take him. It will be a long time before the educational objectives are written to cover only a few of them.

Children's editors know, too, how stories teach even without "teaching." This is what they said in a recent edition of *Writer's Market* to their writers and would-be writers.

> We seriously consider all [juvenile] mss of top professional quality. No heavily moralistic stories.

> . . . we see too many mss that are forced or uninteresting because the writer has tried too hard to make them "educational."

> Story should relate to themes in Christian education (family living, dealing with fears and conflicts, celebrating life in general . . .) without being legalistic or moralistic.

> True or possible plots stressing clean, whole-some Christian character-building ideals, but not preachy.

> Short and lively stories, education for living without moralizing . . . . Character-building ideals should be universal, avoiding the Sunday school image.

In stories, abstract ideas become concrete. Instead of

the abstract idea that God is powerful, we have concrete instances where God made the sun or Jesus told the storm to be still. Instead of the abstract idea that God is good, we have concrete instances where God sends manna to eat or Jesus makes a blind man see.

In stories there is "human meaning." Stories are not simply cold logic, but in them reasoning is invested with emotion. There is more than a proposition such as "We love him, because he first loved us." In a story we see the mothers and children trying to get to Jesus. We empathize with them in their desire, and feel disappointment when the disciples say to go away. And then we feel the graciousness of Jesus as He says to let the children come, and He touches them and blesses them. Little children love a man like that. The story, with its human meaning, leads them to love Jesus.

Stories are close to life. We all know that some of the most effective learning comes from life itself. But in one lifetime we cannot experience everything, so stories can extend our experience.

Stories as Art

Stories as stories—literature—can be called art. Art is more than an ornament of life that could easily be dispensed with. One view has it that art actually leads; instead of imitating life it sets forth that which people follow. Seen in this way, art has power to build up a civilization or to destroy it. If television and movies are full of violence the nation becomes more violent. If a flood of novels portray wife swapping, more people begin practicing wife swapping. If the popular music is sensual and sexual, this affects the moral values and moral life of people who listen to it. Poets, writing about love in the courts of nobility, set up a way of life whose remnants are still with us in such acts as gentlemen opening doors for ladies. While low art can destroy, great art lifts people's thoughts to God; it raises values, raises emotions and actions to a higher plane.

Picture books, stories, and rhymes can be the beginning of presenting the Bible as art. Children should begin having this kind of presentation at a young age. A literature professor, writing not from a Christian perspective but from a secular one, has this to say about Bible content.

> . . . the Bible forms the lowest stratum in the teaching of literature. It should be taught so early and so thoroughly that it sinks straight to the bottom of the mind, where everything that comes along later can settle on it. That, I am aware, is a highly controversial statement, and can be misunderstood in all kinds of ways, so please remember that I'm speaking as a literary critic about the teaching of literature. There are all sorts of secondary reasons for teaching the Bible as literature: the fact that it's so endlessly quoted from and alluded to, the fact that the cadences and phrases of the King James translation are built into our minds and way of thought, the fact that it's full of the greatest and best known stories we have, and so on. There are also the moral and religious reasons for its importance, which are different reasons. But in the particular context in which I'm speaking now, it's the total shape and structure of the Bible which is most important: the fact that it's a continuous narrative beginning with the creation and ending with the Last Judgment, and surveying the whole history of mankind . . . in between (Frye, Northrop, *The Educated Imagination.* Indiana University Press, 1974).

If this is the way of the non-Christian intellectual life, how much more it should be for the Christian. Our children need Bible stories to feed their spirits, to develop their characters, and to lay the foundation for a proper intellectual development.

Stories for Learning

Kindergartners have a keen interest in learning new words. Words standing for concrete things are easiest to learn—shepherd, fisherman, tomb. But even concrete words often have a wide meaning behind them, and children at first will know only parts of the meaning. For instance, the word *king* brings to our adult minds much that we know about reigning nationally, dealing internationally with other leaders, hereditary royalty, and other ideas. A child will know only specific details such as he learns in stories—the king can give orders to other people, the king lives in a big palace, and so forth. But these incomplete understandings are a start toward the fuller understandings that grow as the child grows.

Children seem to especially like long words. When teaching that God made the air, we may wish to use the word *atmosphere* just for the fun of it. Long words are not necessarily harder words. Our task is not to keep all the words short; it is to work at building meaning for the words we teach. And this is one thing stories help us do.

Children may first meet a king when he says that all the people should be counted, so Mary and Joseph go to Bethlehem to be counted. In other stories they meet other kings. Sometimes the kings do good things, sometimes bad. Often they tell people what to do. Children may first meet an angel when he is shiny and bright in the sky and says that Jesus is born. In other stories they will meet other angels. People are usually scared of angels at first; they are not ordinary beings from this world. They often bring a message from God and then leave.

The tabernacle, the temple, disciples, commandments—these and similar Bible words are appropriate for kindergartners to begin learning. Even though they are concrete, words like *angel* take time. We can't teach words like this simply by telling what they are. Children need repeated exposure to the words. They need to hear them, say them, see pictures if it is possible to picture the words, talk about them, and hear stories about them. These last two approaches—the stories and conversations—are ways to put the words in context, to build meaning around them.

Words that we think of as abstract seem more difficult to teach than concrete words, but the approach with these is almost the same. That is, we need concrete examples of the abstraction.

Danny was smashing clay onto a cassette player, when the teacher said in an irritated tone, "Danny! Don't do that. You'll spoil the player."

"I'm sorry, Teacher," Danny replied.

"Okay, I forgive you," said the teacher, and put her arm around Danny. "Now let's see if we can clean it off."

This brief incident with its overtones of emotional, human meaning gives Danny a concrete example of forgiveness at a level he understands. Sin, obedience, and love need to be taught in the same way. These are all learned best in a Christian home, but they can be learned from teachers too.

Here again, stories are needed. In stories these abstract ideas are reduced to concrete instances. God said, "Build a boat," so Noah built a boat. Jesus said, "Let down the net," so Peter let down the net. Others in Bible stories obey God or disobey God. Children who know about obeying parents and teachers now see obedience in a larger context. Stories of present-day children can extend this learning still further.

After children listen to a story you can sometimes spend time talking about it. You won't want to thoroughly dissect every story, but often it is appropriate for you to help the children extract learning from one. Begin your questioning at the fact level. Have the children tell you what happened in the story. If you used a picture book or other kind of visual, let the children look at the pictures and tell you about them. After you see that the children have the facts of the story you can ask other kinds of questions. How do you think the man felt when his sheep was lost? How did he feel when the sheep was found? What would you do?

Did Jesus ever do anything wrong? Did He deserve to die? Why did He die? Could anyone else come to life as Jesus did? Can Jesus give life to other people? Can anyone else do this?

Where did your feet take you today? Where else? If you were lame what would you have done? How would you get to Sunday school class?

The conversation will shift from the story to the children's own feelings and reactions according to the children's responses. As a story's deepest meaning will be different for different children the teacher needs to be sensitive to the various kinds of reactions apparent in the group of children.

Besides using conversation, children can learn the stories by using puppets, roleplaying, pretending one or more parts of the stories, drawing pictures, retelling them with the visuals, and many other kinds of activities which are suggested in good lessons today.

Varieties of Visuals

A picture book has its built-in visualization of the story. The words and pictures blend together, so that all you need is the book and your audience. This is by far the most used and most popular method of presenting stories to kindergartners, everywhere except in the church. Perhaps the high cost of picture books and the unavailability of many Bible stories in this form have slowed the use of picture books in Sunday schools and other church settings. But this has been changing in recent years, as curriculum publishers include visuals in picture book form.

A picture book is not the same as an illustrated Bible story book. The illustrated book ordinarily has a collection of stories, and some pictures to go along with them. There are likely to be large blocks of print, and the whole book is not intended to be read in one sitting. The picture book, on the other hand, is supposed to be read through at one time. There are no large blocks of type, and pictures are at least as important as the type. If you removed either the type or the pictures you probably would not have a comprehensible book. The two blend together to present the story, whereas in the illustrated book the pictures could be removed and the story would still be intact. Suggestions for using picture books and helps for reading them are given in the next chapter.

Another popular type of story visual for young children is the flannelgraph. In Christian education this is probably used most at the present time, whereas in other educational settings the picture book is the most widely used. Publishers have provided a rich choice of these visuals, along with stories, and many teachers have learned how to use them artfully, so they are likely to be a conspicuous fixture for a long time to come, even though other visuals are now growing in popularity. Flannelgraph stories also are discussed more fully in the next chapter.

One of the visuals gaining popularity is puppets. With Bible stories, puppets are best used where conversation is prominent, as in the stories of Moses and the burning bush and Mary and the angel. Two hand puppets or two stick puppets can carry on these conversation stories without need for stage or scenery or other props.

Puppets have other classroom uses, such as conversing with the children, handing out awards and so on. And with stories there are two major ways to use them. One is for the puppet to be the storyteller. The lovable animal puppet, or the grandpa puppet, or "Miss Susie the Storylady" can become a regular storyteller in the classroom.

The second use is for several puppets to act out a story. It takes an artful script writer to work out a story which fits this medium. When choosing published stories you need to watch out for the kind that contain long, preachy speeches. You will need a faster-moving, conversational-style dialogue. Another kind of script to avoid is the non-story, "teaching" one. In some scripts child puppets talk about love or forgiveness as though they were seventh graders working on a vocabulary assignment. A far superior kind of script is the story which illustrates the love or forgiveness, showing it in action. Here is an example from *Puppets Help Teach* (Warner, Dianne, Accent-B/P Publications). Sally and Nancy don't just talk about love, but in the story they show love to the new girl. This is concrete—love in action.

SALLY AND NANCY LEARN FROM DAVID AND MEPHIBOSHETH

SCRIPTURE: II Samuel 9
CHARACTERS: Sally and Nancy
PROPS: Two bracelets attached to the backs of Sally and Nancy with thread (shiny plastic, if possible, to look like "hula hoops." These are held up by the "hands" of Sally and Nancy).

SALLY: Hi, Nancy.
NANCY: Hi, Sally, do you have your hula hoop?
SALLY: Yes, do you?
NANCY: Um hmmm. I'm sure glad school is out—I couldn't wait to try it out.
SALLY: Is it new?
NANCY: Yes, I just got it on Saturday. I saved my

allowance for a whole month.

SALLY: What tricks can you do?

NANCY: Well, I can try to do "ocean waves." [*Nancy makes an effort to get hula hoop to go around her waist. Of course, it won't because it is attached with thread on the back of her dress, but it will appear as if she is trying.*]
I can't do it. Can you?

SALLY: It's really hard, but I think I can do Saturn's Rings.

NANCY: Let me see.
[*Sally again "tries"—to no avail of course.*]

SALLY: This isn't my day.

NANCY: Hey, Sally, look over there. . . .

SALLY: Where?

NANCY: There's that new girl at school.

SALLY: You mean, the one with the crippled leg?

NANCY: Yeah, she's so shy, she just sits around all the time. She never plays or anything.

SALLY: I know.

NANCY: Well, come on, let's practice. I'll give it another try. [*Nancy "tries" again.*]

SALLY: Nancy, you're as bad as I am. [*Laughs.*]

NANCY: [*Laughs.*] I know.
[*Silence.*]

SALLY: What's the matter?

NANCY: I just feel guilty standing here, having fun, when that girl is there watching us.

SALLY: She can't do things like we can, 'cause of her leg.

NANCY: I know. I feel sorry for her. Look at her—doesn't it make you want to do something for her?

SALLY: Just like David in the Bible?

NANCY: David?

SALLY: Yes, don't you remember? How he felt sorry for little Mephibosheth?

NANCY: Oh, yeah, I remember. Maybe we can do something for her too. What is her name?

SALLY: Her name is Anna.

NANCY: Oh, well, what could we do—you know, to show her that we care . . . and that we want to play with her?

SALLY: First of all, we have to think of something she could play.

NANCY: How about Tiddly-winks or Jacks or something?

SALLY: Hey, Jacks is a good idea.

NANCY: You just have to sit down for that.

SALLY: Right. I've got some Jacks at home.

NANCY: Let's go see if she wants to play.

SALLY: Okay. Come on.

[*Sally and Nancy exit.*]

Here, from the same book, is an example of a Bible story in puppet form.

THE SHEPHERD AND THE LOST SHEEP

SCRIPTURE: Luke 15:1-7
CHARACTERS: shepherd, lamb
PROPS: A furry white lamb cut from cardboard with cotton glued onto him. Small dry branches.
SETTING:Lamb is stuck in the branches at one end of the stage.

SHEPHERD:

Has anybody seen my little lost sheep? Have you? I've counted my sheep three times and there are only 99 sheep. There are 100 sheep, but I can only find 99! I've got to find my little lamb. There is no one else who will look for him but me. If I don't find him, a lion might get him, or a bear might kill him.

Stevie [*Substitute name of child in audience*], have you seen my little lost lamb?

Toni, have you seen him?

I'll look over here in the meadow. No, he's not here.

I'll look over behind these rocks. No, he's not here.

What was that?

Baa. [*Faintly in distance.*]

Did you hear something? [*He asks audience.*]

Listen! Baaa, baaa, baaa.

I hear my little sheep. I'm coming. I'm coming. I'll find you!

Baaa, baaa, baaa.

Oh, little one, I'm coming. I'll save you.

He must be here somewhere. [*He gets closer to the lamb.*]

There he is—caught in the briars of that bush. Here little sheep—come on. [*He lifts him up.*] I've got you now. Don't be afraid. Oh, poor little lamb, you're so cold and afraid. Here, I'll hold you close! Oh, you have a little cut on your leg. I'll put healing oil on it. I'll take care of you and never let you get hurt again. Come on, let's go back to the meadow.

[*He exits holding sheep in his arms.*]

Drawings are another visual which can be used with certain story situations. Artists may use colored chalk and draw elaborate pictures, but if you are untalented at drawing you can still use this medium. Your drawings might be termed diagrams instead of true pictures, but they can be effective. For these visuals, you may use chalk on a chalkboard, charcoal or felt pen on large newsprint paper, or you may draw on the acetate of an overhead projector.

A chalk story needs to be specially written or prepared for this medium. If you are preparing your own from a Bible story, you will find its best use is in presenting the setting of the story. You can use the drawing for the setting, and then read or tell the rest of the story with no visuals.

This system, by the way, works well with ready-made pictures too. You can show the pictures, talk about them, and then tell the story with no further visuals. The rationale for this will be explained in the next chapter.

Here is an example of a chalk drawing used to set the story. It is intended to give the feeling of a town (Capernaum), separated from other towns—not the space concept involved, but the "event" that Jesus preached and healed in a town. This is to help build the idea stated in the closing two paragraphs of the story. The storyteller who relies on words may feel that "walking, walking" and other phrases in this story do the job themselves. But the teacher who believes in visuals will feel better with this illustrated, as the chalk drawing does.

Long ago Jesus was living in the world. One day He went walking, walking till at last He came to a big lake.

On the lake some men were fishing. Jesus called the men to follow Him. Then Jesus and the fishermen went walking, walking, till they came into a little town beside the lake.

And in the town they went walking,

walking till they came to the synagogue. Other people were walking to the synagogue too. People came up one street and up the other street. People came from all the houses and went into the synagogue, just as people do today when it's time for church. Jesus and the fishermen went into the synagogue, too.

Inside the synagogue the people worshiped God. And then they needed a teacher. So someone asked Jesus to be the teacher. Jesus stood up and read from God's Book, and He preached and explained what the Book meant.

The people were surprised. One man said, "This Teacher knows more than all the other teachers."

Another man said, "Yes, we never had a teacher like this before." All the people liked to have Jesus for their teacher.

One man in the synagogue had an evil spirit. The evil spirit hurt the man and made him cry out. So Jesus said to the evil spirit, "Come out of the man." The evil spirit came out and the man was all well.

The people were surprised again. One man asked, "What is this new thing that Jesus can do?"

Another man said, "We never saw a man do that before."

Then the people left the synagogue. They went walking, walking down one street and down the other street and to their houses again. In one house a man said to his family, "Jesus knows more than all the other teachers."

In another house a man said to his friend, "Jesus can make people well."

People talked like that in all the houses in the little town beside the big lake. And soon everyone knew what Jesus could do. So they began to bring the sick people to Jesus. They brought sick children and sick mothers and sick friends. They brought the people who had evil spirits, too. And Jesus made the people well.

The people said to Jesus, "Please stay in our town."

But Jesus said, "I must go into the other towns and preach in them, too."

So Jesus and the fishermen went walking, walking to all the towns. And Jesus preached and made the people well.

Participation Stories

As a change from visuals, sometimes you can have the children participate in various ways. The simplest way to do this is to have the children join on certain words, such as saying "Whoo" for the wind, or saying "Clop, clop" as the donkey travels. The children need to listen closely for the cue words that tell them when to join you, thus their concentration is heightened.

In planning this kind of story, you need to be sure the children's parts come in often enough that they will get the full pleasure from them. Some Bible stories, with their repetition, are especially suited to this form. In the creation story the children may repeat the line "and the evening and the morning were the first day," ". . . the second day," and so forth. When Moses goes before Pharaoh ten times he says, "Let my people go," and Pharaoh says, "I will not let you go," until the last time, when he changes his mind. Stories that do not have repetition in their original form can be made to have repetition. For instance, Noah listens for the rain and "Pit, pat" it is coming down. The next day he listens and "Pit, pat," it is still coming down. This continues for many days and then there is no pit, pat, but Noah hears the wind, "Whoo."

The participation lines are even more fun if they are made more elaborate and poem-like. One story about Balaam and his donkey capitalizes on the "threeness" found naturally in the story. Balaam mounts his donkey three times, and the children step their feet in time as they say,

> "Clop, clop, cloppity-clop.
> Hurry, little donkey. Don't you stop."

But the donkey stops three times and the children hit one arm with their hand, and say,

> "Wham, wham, whamity-wham.
> Hurry, little donkey, as fast as you can."

Often the participation line can emphasize a major teaching of the story. This is really quite easy to do, as long as you remember to give the children enough opportunities to repeat their line. Here is an example of how such a story might be arranged. The capitalized portions show where the children join the storyteller. They need to listen for the cue that tells them each time Jesus is going to speak.

> One day Jesus was walking along by the shore of the sea. There He saw Peter and Andrew catching some fish with their nets. Jesus said, "COME, FOLLOW ME." Then He said, "I will teach you how to be fishers of men."

Peter and Andrew left their nets and they followed Jesus. Then Jesus had two disciples—Peter and Andrew.

Jesus walked farther along the shore of the sea. Soon He came to where James and John were working. They were in a boat mending the holes in their fishing nets. When Jesus saw them, He said, "COME, FOLLOW ME."

James and John left the boat and they followed Jesus. Then Jesus had four disciples—Peter and Andrew, and James and John.

Another day when Jesus was walking along He came to Matthew sitting at a table where he collected taxes from the people. When Jesus saw Matthew He said, "COME, FOLLOW ME."

Matthew got up from the table and followed Jesus. Then Jesus had five disciples—Peter and Andrew, James and John, and Matthew.

Later on Jesus chose some other men. He said to them, "COME, FOLLOW ME." Jesus kept saying, "COME, FOLLOW ME," until He had twelve disciples in all.

The twelve disciples followed Jesus, and Jesus was their teacher. He told them about God and about Heaven. He told them all the good things to know.

The good things are in the Bible so we can know them too. In the Bible Jesus talks to you. Jesus says, "COME, FOLLOW ME."

Using children as "living visuals" is another kind of participation. In the story above, you could choose two children to sit apart from the others and be Peter and Andrew. Choose two more to be James and John, and a fifth to be Matthew. As you tell the story you can call each of these, and then others, to follow you to a certain place. This will visually demonstrate the calling of the twelve disciples and the responding of those called. Children of kindergarten age are usually extremely interested in numbers and counting, and they will love to count the twelve afterward, to see if you were right.

In the story of the good Samaritan one of your boys could lie on the floor and be the injured Jew. When the appropriate time comes, others could be the priest and the Levite to walk by without helping, and the Samaritan who stops to help.

Rhythm instruments add another dimension to participation stories. Instead of just tapping feet and clapping hands, the kinds of sounds available are greatly multiplied. These stories are fun to do the first time, and they are also good for repeating in the manner of songs or action rhymes. So the story may be an abbreviated form of the full story as you tell it—a form written especially for rhythm instruments.

Here is an example of a "sound story" written for use with instruments, or with alternate sounds if instruments are not available. To gain a better appreciation of how these stories affect the children's thinking, you need to imagine yourself in the place of one child with one instrument listening for his proper time to play. Before reading the story to a group of children you would have them practice playing their sounds at the proper cues.

BUILDING THE TABERNACLE

Cue	*Instrument*	*Alternate sound*
wood	*sticks (hit), or wood blocks*	*Knock on the table or chairs.*
gold	*triangles*	*Say, "Tinkle, tinkle."*
brass	*cymbal*	*Clap.*
thread	*sticks (rub)*	*Rub hands.*
God was there.	*drum*	*Stomp feet.*

65

Moses said to the people, "The Lord wants Bezaleel to see that the tabernacle is made right. Bezaleel can teach men how to make things out of wood (*tap, tap*), and gold (*tinkle, tinkle*), and brass (*crash*). Bezaleel and his helper can teach people how to weave cloth out of smooth thread (*rub, rub*), and how to embroider designs on the cloth with colored thread" *(rub, rub)*.

Moses finished telling the people what the Lord wanted. Then Bezaleel and his helper and the people began to make the tabernacle exactly as God said to make it. They made boards out of wood (*tap, tap*), and covered them with gold (*tinkle, tinkle*). Bezaleel made a table out of wood (*tap, tap*), and covered it with gold (*tinkle, tinkle*). He made a lamp out of pure gold (*tinkle, tinkle*). And he made an altar out of wood (*tap, tap*) and covered it with brass *(crash)*. The people wove curtains out of smooth thread (*rub, rub*). And they embroidered designs on the curtains with colored thread" *(rub, rub)*.

The people finished making all the things and brought them to Moses. Moses put up the boards of wood (*tap, tap*) that were covered with gold (*tinkle, tinkle*). Over the boards Moses hung animal skins to make a tent. On the right side Moses put the table which was made of wood (*tap, tap*) and covered with gold (*tinkle, tinkle*). On the left side he put the lamp which was made of pure gold (*tinkle, tinkle*). On the outside he put the altar made of wood (*tap, tap*) and covered with brass (*crash*). Then Moses hung up the curtains which were made of smooth thread *(rub, rub*) and embroidered with colored thread (*rub, rub*).

After that a cloud covered the tabernacle, and God's bright light filled the tabernacle. And

Moses could not go in because God was there
(*boom, boom, boom*).

READING CHECK

1. Stories can teach things we may never think to
teach.   T   F
2. The "human meaning" of stories gives them a power
beyond straight, didactic teaching.   T   F
3. Long words are difficult for young children to
learn.   T   F
4. A picture book is not the same thing as an illustrated
story book.   T   F
5. Children need a visual with every story.   T   F

Answers: 1—T, 2—T, 3—F, 4—T, 5—F

4 More About Stories

- *The Case for Reading Stories*
- *How to Read Stories and Picture Books*
- *Telling Stories*

The Case for Reading Stories

One day a four-year-old said, "Grandma, I want a story." So Grandma began to tell him a favorite story, which she had read to him often. "No. Not that way," the little boy said, and he ran to get the book. "Now, tell it this way."

That is the first argument in the case for reading stories. Young children like their stories to have the right words. It would never do for the wolf to say, "I'm gonna blow hard until I make your house fall down." No. The wolf has to say, "I'll huff and I'll puff till I blow your house in." Anything else is just not the right story.

We believe in singing songs over and over—the very same words and the very same tune—for years and years of our children's growing time. We do the same with fingerplays or action rhymes; after we have learned a few that we think are good we do not hesitate to use them repeatedly. But when it comes to stories we are likely to say, "Oh, they've heard that." But if a story is in the right words children want to hear it over again, and they want to recognize their favorite lines and not have them mangled, as the grandmother did with her four-year-old's story. We could help our children to know many Bible stories as well as they know "Jesus Loves Me" if we would take this approach in their early years.

Besides the repetition advantage, there are still other reasons why teachers should read stories. One is that children need opportunities to form their own mental images. This is especially true of a TV generation. Children who always have images flashed on a screen or a flannelboard in front of them are deprived of opportunity to develop their own image-making skills, and this is an important aspect of intelligence. Good ability in imagery is needed for problem solving and creative thinking at high levels, as well as for richness in everyday life. Kindergarten children can begin to develop this ability and older children should continue it. Perhaps we would have more "readers" among our children if more of them learned in this way how reading can transport them in their imaginations to all kinds of places and times.

The best way to encourage children to become readers is for the adults around them to read. In kindergartens the teachers will read to them; summers the librarian will read to them; and at home most parents will read to them. What does it say to children if they come to our Sunday schools and Bible schools and we do not read to them? Does it say that other stories are for reading, but Bible stories are not?

Teachers who learn that it is all right to read stories are usually very happy about this. It takes much less preparation to read a story well than it does to tell it well. Good storytellers practice and develop their skill just as musicians do. And a repertoire of prepared stories rarely includes enough to use one every Sunday of the year. So with the demands of regular teaching, if one believes he must tell stories instead of reading them he lets down on his standards. His stories are not arranged as well as they could be; and the words are not chosen nearly as carefully as the writer's, whose story he is using; and the delivery is not his best. But if that teacher becomes convinced of the value of reading stories, a great burden is lifted from his teaching load. He can use the writer's carefully chosen words, he can enjoy the story along with his children, and he can use his leftover preparation time on more important matters.

For those who ask, "What about the eye contact and the direct communication, that is supposed to make storytelling superior to story reading?" the answer is we really don't know. At college level there have been many research studies comparing various methods of presenting information—lecture, discussion, film, programmed learning, TV, radio, computer assisted instruction. When these numerous studies are taken together the overall conclusion is that "any teaching method is about as 'good' as any other" when the content coverage is the same *(The Psychology of Teaching Methods,* National Society for the Study of Education, University of Chicago Press). Those who compiled these studies have concluded that it is time to quit comparing teaching methods and to turn to studies of how each method can be used to best advantage.

Though college level studies do not actually tell us about the younger ages, these data may at least hint that there is a possibility that reading stories and telling stories do not really differ in the amount of learning they produce. We have no research data either way. And, if we are to take a lesson from the college studies, it might not even pay us to research reading versus telling stories. It might be better to focus on ways to use both of the methods to best advantage.

How to Read Stories and Picture Books

First, we must make it clear that we are considering here the reading of stories and picture books. We are not advocating reading a Bible lesson to children. Some published lessons contain stories which may be either read or told, according to preference. Other lessons do not present Bible stories as stories. They often use a story as a base, and intersperse it with sermonizing and other "teaching." Those Bible lessons are not intended for reading aloud. But such lessons could be augmented with a session of story reading.

In reading stories one of the most important considerations is good use of the voice. It is not necessary to dramatize, and probably not good to do so unless a teacher has a special talent for that. But a reader should learn to use normal voice inflections for expression. Inexperience or "stage fright" often cause teachers to raise the pitch of their voices. And the rising pitch tends to excite the children, whereas a low pitch tends to calm them.

Inexperienced readers may also read too fast. This makes it difficult for the children to hear all the words, and also to follow the thought. On the other hand, too slow reading gives the mind time to wander and lose interest in the story. A good pace will usually be just slightly slower than conversational speed—a speed which allows each word enough time for enunciation, but not so much time as to sound affected. A natural sound is the goal here. But remember that, as you can see and read the words, you can take in thoughts more rapidly than your listeners, who are depending upon the sense of hearing and upon their internal images. Variations in speed can be used for effect, just as variations in voice inflection. Excitement, suspense and other moods can be heightened by reading faster or slower. If the reader is living in the story and enjoying it along with his listeners, his own ear will tell him what to do—he just does what comes naturally. At least it comes naturally after a little practice.

With young children, picture book reading is very effective and it would pay us to make more use of it in Christian education. Books to use for groups should have pictures with outlines and composition clear enough for all in the group to see, and there should be good balance between pictures and text so that they move along together. Solid pages of type will not work, as the children want things to move and pages to turn faster than that. The youngest kindergartners will like "naming" books, in which they participate in naming the picture on each page; and "surprise" books in which they try to guess what will come when the page is turned. Older children will like books with more plot. Three general types of picture books are: 1) stories with plot and action, 2) explorations of an idea or mood, and 3) participation or game-like books. In any one reading session all three types can be used and, except with the very youngest children, the story type should dominate.

A session of picture books can begin at about fifteen or twenty minutes length for inexperienced listeners and can extend longer than that within a few weeks as the group becomes accustomed to it. The reader should have a planned program of stories, as well as a couple of alternates. The alternates are to pick up in case a change of pace is needed. If a long story begins to drag, the reader can condense and skip and quickly bring it to a close, and then read a different type of book or else use a fingerplay or other short interlude. With children of five and older the reader can sometimes read stories unaccompanied by pictures, as these children will enjoy listening to stories and forming their own mental pictures to go with them. A longer book is best used at the beginning of the program.

The children can sit in chairs or on the floor. If on the floor, they can be taught to put their hands on their hips and to check whether they have enough elbow room, and they can be taught to keep their hands on their own laps. A familiar rhyme called "Open, Shut Them" helps with this teaching. They also can be taught to sit Indian style. These precautions help keep children from interfering with one another's attention. Arrange the children in a shallow semicircle; there need not be only one row.

Sometimes it works well to have a row of chairs in back and let those who wish to sit on the floor be in front. If there are any distractions in the room, such as another class, traffic passing through, bright sun shining in a window and so forth, arrange the children so their backs are toward the distraction and the teacher is facing it.

The reader should be on a low chair and should hold the book just slightly above the heads of children in the front row. The book should be held so that the children can see the pictures and the reader must learn to see the words as best she can. It may take a little practice at first to work this out, but a reader familiar with the book often needs only to glance at it. The pages can be turned from either top or bottom in a manner that does not move the arm across the pictures. The reader should never turn the book toward herself or himself to read a page and then toward the children to show a picture. This destroys the wholeness of the book; picture and words must go together. If your group is large you may slowly swing the book from side to side so that all may see well. But avoid small, jerky movements, which are distracting.

All the discipline techniques that teachers generally apply in group work with small children will apply here. Children's interruptions should be handled as unobtrusively as possible, so as to keep the story moving and not let the distraction grow into something big. If a very immature child does not sit with the group but wanders elsewhere, the reader can ignore him if the group can.

Using a child's name can help bring his attention back to the story. For instance: "And after that, Carol, God said 'Let the waters gather together in one place.'" Sometimes a look only is needed. Sometimes you may have to move a child. Simply say, "I think you'll be able to listen better over here." Don't scold and lecture and make an example of him.

If a child interrupts with a comment about the story, nod to him and say "Yes" or any brief, appropriate comment. Recognition will usually satisfy him and quiet him. If a child interrupts with an irrelevant comment about his dog at home or anything else on his mind, try the same technique of a quick recognition and then back to the story. Do this quickly so other children will not have time to enter in with news items about their own dogs.

The main principle in all of these suggestions is to make every effort to keep the story going. Do not break its continuity by making major discipline situations out of these occurrences.

After a story session which has gone well the reader will sense something of what has happened between her and the children. This in itself is an evaluation of the experience. Many books will be read for their "story" value and not as takeoff points for other learning, as described in the previous section. When a story is read in this way it is not necessary to get response from the children. If you say, "Did you like the book?" most children will answer, "Yes," and that is the end of that. Whereas if you leave them with their personal feelings and impressions they will go much deeper. The question only serves to teach the children a shallow level of evaluating. A good ending is simply to say, "And that was the story of David and Goliath," and then move on to the next story or activity. Children are not well able to express their deep responses to stories. You may occasionally see a tiny part of their response emerge in words, but the far larger part is happening in the mind and heart. You need to be satisfied that it is there, and not feel that the children have only learned what you can see on the surface. The deeper learning will flower forth in the months to come.

Telling Stories

There are several good books on storytelling and most local libraries will have at least one of these. Any teacher who wishes to improve his or her storytelling abilities should study one or more of these books.

The outstanding impression one gains from these accomplished storytellers is that storytelling is an art. As a singer thoroughly masters his song before presenting it, so a storyteller must master his story. He needs perfect knowledge of his story; he needs to know it so well he cannot possibly forget parts. He must not only know it, but he must *be* it. No one tells a story well until that story has become a part of himself.

An artist storyteller must have a sensitive ear for language—a fine feeling for words, for their sounds and infinite nuances of meaning. He must love words as the musician loves tone and melody. They are his means of communication.

The story is the message, the words are the medium, the teller is the artist. The art of storytelling is not drama. Dramatization is something else. Storytelling is a simple, direct sharing of the story. In his sincerity, the artist storyteller's natural gestures and natural facial expressions will communicate that story which he knows so perfectly and loves so well that it has become a part of him.

In telling stories to young children there is a further qualification. A fine feel for words and a love of the story are not enough in themselves. The artist teacher must study the minds of young children. He must observe their own use of words, and be able to communicate in ordinary things so that he can communicate his story appropriately.

The matters of room arrangement, discipline and so forth, can be handled similarly to the suggestions given in the previous section. Stories can be repeated, as children ask for them. Stories can be told for their own sake and not be limited to one story around which a lesson is built.

Visuals are a controversial matter. The true artist

storyteller insists that words are his medium and he trusts his words to do the work. He points out that it introduces confusion into the children's minds to be watching you, listening to your words and following the story, and at the same time have to look at a picture to see what someone else thinks a particular happening looks like. That picture may be entirely different from the one the child is imaging internally. A child cannot be expected to do so many things at one time. A storyteller with this view agrees that pictures are fine for children— even valuable—but not while they are caught up in a story experience.

"Flannelgraph teachers" who have come this far are likely screaming their objections by now, at least inwardly. Working in Christian education is a large army of teachers trained in the art of telling flannelgraph stories. Many of them feel that all stories must have visuals.

The argument for visuals given to us teachers is derived more from teaching as a "science" than from storytelling as an art. When we hear that children remember more of what they see than of what they hear, and if this information is accompanied by a percentage figure that comes from a research project, the scientific sound is so impressive that it seems heresy to question it. But we will commit the heresy here, and at least examine the claim.

When specific figures are quoted telling how much people remember on seeing something versus hearing the same information, unless someone is passing on hearsay, the figures have to come from a specific research study. They are not from a generalized learning law. And, unfortunately, most writers who quote such figures do not give enough information about the study to help us know how applicable their figures might be to our own situation. For instance, one such study concerned salesmen in a training meeting who were given certain information on a graph projected for all to see, and a control group who were given the same information orally in their meeting. When tested on the information those who saw the graph remembered a higher percentage of facts than those who did not.

These results have been quoted widely and applied to all ages and all kinds of Bible teaching. But stories are quite different from sales data, and kindergartners are quite different from adults. Also, there are many other factors that should be considered if we really want to know what helps remembering. Some of these are the way the material was organized, the meaningfulness to the hearers, whether or not a question was raised in the salesmen's minds before it was answered either by the visual or by oral means. The hearing and seeing are only two of many factors.

You perhaps can think of a story which you read or heard and have never forgotten. And you no doubt have seen many stories on TV which you have long since forgotten. From this you can understand that it is not the seeing versus the hearing which is crucial, but other factors, most probably the meaningfulness of the story to you at the time you heard it.

So the storyteller artist says, "No visuals to distract," and the flannelgraph teacher says, "Always use visuals." The reason for this enigma is probably that the flannelgraph teachers are more artists than they suspect, and not really scientists. When their stories are successful, it is not simply because they have visuals to help the children to remember, but it is because they have made an art form of the flannelgraph story. Story and pictures are integrated, as in picture books, and they need each other. A story without this kind of integration, which has pictures added to it for scientific reasons, is not a fully successful story.

When older children, or even young teachers, are questioned about their memories of flannelgraph stories, their answers differ widely. One will say, "It never interested me. Those little things on the board that the teacher kept handling." Another will say, "I remember the first time I heard a flannelgraph story. I kept my eyes glued to the board. I had never heard anything so wonderful." There are differences, of course, in children's readiness to obtain meaning from any particular story, but surely also some of these variations in reaction are due to the story itself. Some stories are made for flannelgraph; they are an artistic, integrated whole. Other stories are better told without visuals appended to them, and some are better read.

With Bible stories sometimes the flannelgraph picture can build piece by piece as the story progresses. Creation stories fit this pattern. Sometimes the flannelgraph can parade its figures in a row across the board, such as when Adam names the animals or the animals come to the ark. Sometimes the figures can show story sequence, each part in the sequence remaining in place. An example of this is the cross, the closed tomb and the open tomb. Such story signposts can help the children retell the story themselves after the teacher tells it. Another example is an angel, John the Baptist, and Jesus. The angel said John is coming, John said Jesus is coming, and Jesus came.

Possibly the most unneeded flannelgraph visuals are when a man talks to someone here, then he goes to talk to someone there, and people move about from place to place. One reason these do nothing for some stories is that they are the least important part of the story. For example, in the story of the Emmaus Road event it is the conversation and the fact that Jesus is alive again that are important. But the conversation cannot be visualized and it is a poor substitute to show the walking instead. It is possible, though, for an artful storyteller to build the story around the appearance and disappearance of Jesus, which make concrete the fact that He is alive and in His resurrection body.

Children's own visualizations of this and other events may be more dramatic than the paper figures on the board. When it comes to angels and Heaven and other things we are never sure how to visualize, it would be a good idea if we left children to their own devices more often. If every time we say *angel* we put up a paper angel, we are likely to stifle children's imagery of awesome angels, rather than stimulate it.

Another problem with flannelgraph stories showing people moving from place to place has to do with visualization of space. If someone walks to another town it is quite an advanced mental feat to visualize that kind of space. Young children have not developed this ability well. Walking a figure across a board, or removing him and changing the scenery do not help in this—in fact, they confuse. Stories need to be arranged so that they do not depend on advanced space (or time) concepts. This is part of the art of the storyteller.

Here is an example of a story written especially for flannelgraph. In this, Rodney learns about using the eyes God gave him. As Rodney looks at the chocolate cake and tries to think of luscious, gooey ways to describe it, your children, too, have a chocolate cake to look at. Their mouths can water as their own senses get involved in this story.

RODNEY AND HIS EYES

	Rodney sat on the floor watching TV.
Place gun at left.	He saw a man shoot a gun. Then a car chased another car. The cars were going too fast and it was scary. Pretty soon a
Wrecked car.	car crashed and some people got killed.
	Everything on TV moved very fast and Rodney kept watching. A man
Lady.	caught a lady and the lady screamed.

80

When it was over Mother said, "Time for bed now, Rodney." Rodney took a long time getting undressed and eating some crackers. He didn't want to go to bed; he wanted to watch TV with Mother and Daddy. But at last Rodney was in bed all by himself.

The dark room was scary. Rodney thought he could see a smashed-up car and the hurt people on the road. He saw a man sneaking up and a lady open her mouth to scream. All the things that happened on TV Rodney imagined he could see again in his dark room. He pulled the covers over his face to try to hide the pictures but they were still there.

Rodney heard a noise. He thought, "Maybe that's a man with a gun." So Rodney didn't move. He hardly breathed at all, and his heart inside him pounded hard. Rodney listened to see if the man came closer, but he couldn't hear a sound. Rodney waited and waited, and he was still too scared to move.

After a while he heard the sound again; then Rodney yelled as loud as he could. In an instant Mother's arms were around Rodney and the light was on.

"He was going to get me," sobbed Rodney.

"Who was going to get you?" asked Mother.

Rodney cried harder. "The man," he said. "And he had a gun and the lady screamed and the car crashed, and ... and ..."

"Oh, that was on the TV show," said

Mother. "That's not here in your room."

"I'm scared," said Rodney. "May I sleep in your bed?"

"For a little while you can sleep in my bed," said Mother. And she carried Rodney just like he was a little baby again.

Remove
gun, car
and lady
from
flannel-
board.

The next night Rodney started to turn on the TV. Mother said, "No, Rodney. Don't watch those bad things tonight. Let's play a game. Let's think of three good things to look at before bedtime. You start. Now what's the best thing you can think of to look at?"

Rodney thought and thought. Then suddenly he remembered something. "I know, Mother. The best thing is that chocolate cake you made today."

Mother laughed. "You're supposed to think of something to look at and not something to taste. But I'll give you a piece of the cake. You can look at it and eat it, too."

Place cake
on the left.

Mother began to cut the cake. "What does it look like, Rodney?" she asked.

"Mm-mm," said Rodney. "It looks like chocolate cake."

"What else can you say about the way it looks?" asked Mother.

Rodney began to think. "It looks good. The frosting looks gooey. The cake looks brown, and crumbly, and chocolate. That's all I can think of."

"Now you can taste it," said Mother. And she set the cake on the table for Rodney.

When Rodney finished eating, Mother said, "Now it's my turn to think of something good to see. Here's your sweater because we're going outside."

Rodney and Mother went out into the yard. Then Mother said, "Look up at the moon and tell me what you see."

Moon.

"I see the moon," said Rodney.

"Tell me what the moon looks like," said Mother.

Rodney had to think again. "It looks yellow," he said. "And it looks like it was round but part of it is gone. And it looks far away. I wish I could go to the moon."

"Maybe some day you will," said Mother. "Now it's your turn to think of something good to look at."

Rodney and Mother started to walk into the house again. Rodney said, "I know what to look at next."

"What is it?" asked Mother.

Rodney said, "It's the picture in my Sunday school book. The man couldn't see the moon till Jesus fixed his eyes. Then he could see everything."

Mother said, "All right, you get ready for bed. Then we will look at the picture and I'll read you the story too."

This time Rodney got undressed in a hurry and brushed his teeth and hopped into bed. Then he called, "I'm ready, Mother."

Book.

Mother came with the book. Rodney showed her the picture and told her all about the man. He said, "Now read it to me, please."

After the story Mother turned out the light and went away. Rodney looked at the moon through his window. Then he thought about Jesus being in the room, and Jesus was going to take care of him all night.

READING CHECK

1. Research has proved that children learn better if there is constant eye contact with the teacher during a lesson.　T　F

2. It confuses children if they have more than one story during a class session.　T　F

3. Teachers cannot see all the results of their teaching in the changed behavior of the children.　T　F

4. It is probably not possible to write behavioral objectives for the deepest learning that happens during stories.　T　F

5. It is all right to repeat stories children have heard before.　T　F

6. There is a law of learning that tells us children learn more through their eyegate than other ways.　T　F

Answers: 1—F, 2—F, 3—F, 4—T, 5—T, 6—F

5 Teaching with Art

- *Developmental Stages of Art*
- *God, the Source and Goal of Art*
- *Creativity Versus Directed Art*
- *Art as Learning and Growing*

Developmental Stages of Art

Teachers find it enormously helpful to understand the stages children pass through as their art ability is developing. If we would be guides along the way, if we would make the best use of art activities in our Bible teaching, it is essential to have this understanding. It does no good to say, "Draw a picture of today's story," if the children are not in the picture—or representative—stage of development. A description of the major stages follows.

Manipulative stage. This is the stage children must begin with when they first use any new art media. In this stage they experiment with manipulating the crayons, paint, clay or other materials. At first the manipulation is quite random. The child with a crayon makes scratches, just trying it out. Later his marks become more controlled and purposeful. There may be rhythm in what he does, and he tries to make different kinds of marks—sweeping, bold, circular, and so on.

The child at this stage is very happy in his work. Once he has become used to the kindergarten classroom he is normally a social person. He laughs and talks with others. He handles the clay of other children and makes marks on their papers, and he seems not to resent their additions to his own work.

When the child first tries a paint brush he usually handles it as a crayon, making lines rather than areas of color. But his experimentations later lead him to produce areas of color, which then are sometimes outlined with another color. Some children try out different effects the brush can achieve—stippling or splattering, for instance. The child begins to repeat and practice various shapes he has made.

Through these earlier stages the child has no theme or title for his work, but the day comes when he sees a face in his circle. He may add two eyes and say, "It's a man," or "It's me." Since his painted shapes are often boxlike, he may say, "It's a window." Sometimes the movement rather than the shape gives a title to the work. The child may swirl his crayon around, saying, "Zoom, zoom." It is an airplane zooming around. Or he may dab, dab, dab his brush across the paper and say it's a boy walking. If you are not there when it happens you may wonder what relation the marks have to the title the child gives you.

With three-dimensional media the child goes through the same progression. With clay, for instance, he at first just squeezes it through his fingers. Later he makes more controlled movements, rolling it into lengths, shaping it into balls, and so forth. With blocks, he simply stacks in no particular order and then knocks down. Later he learns how to put larger blocks at the bottom or in other ways make more orderly arrangements.

No matter what the media, there will first be a manipulative stage, and that stage includes these three phases.

1. Random manipulation.
2. Controlled manipulation.

3. Named or planned manipulation.

The three phases overlap, and the ages at which children pass through them will of course vary. If children are supplied with art media they can begin the random manipulation phase at age 2 or even earlier. But with each new kind of media they will have to go through this stage no matter what their age. Even as an adult, if you have a new felt pen you are likely to try out a few marks with it before making your poster. Many of your four- and five-year-old children will be in the named manipulation phase, and some will be beyond it. Perhaps many of your six-year-olds will have progressed beyond the manipulative stage and be developing into the representative stage.

Children are learning during this manipulative stage. They are often completely absorbed with the fun of playing with the materials and trying out various things to do with them. Their interest in the material is so great that they fail to be interested in what they produce.

Teachers unaware of this stage of development sometimes run into trouble at this point. If the teacher is intent on the production of a basket for baby Moses while the child has been carried away with the fun of sweeping paint across his paper, there are bound to be problems. The child is limited by his maturity level and he cannot change to satisfy the teacher. So it is the teacher who must change his expectations.

This manipulative stage is normal for young children and they should not be forced into the next stage before they are ready for it. What the children need at this time is plenty of opportunity to work with materials. The materials themselves are motivating, so the teacher needs to do little else in the way of motivation except provide materials and a minimum of guidance in their use.

Representative stage. This is sometimes called the stage of symbols, and many kindergarten children enter into this stage. A child arrives at his first symbol through the named-manipulative phase. That is, when the child first looks at one of his circles and says "It's me" he is moving into the representative stage. He next comes to control his representations and make them at will.

The first symbol a child develops is usually a human being. This symbol may in the beginning have only a head with eyes, and perhaps a mouth or a nose. Later the child will add body parts which have the most meaning for him. Usually arms and legs will appear before a main body, or trunk. The child continues to refine his human being, differentiating for sex by distinction in hair or clothing or both. Details in clothing and small body parts such as fingers gradually appear. He comes to draw not merely a man but policeman, pastor, daddy. He will draw mother, teacher, and specific children.

The first symbol is not always a human being; it may be a flower, animal, piece of furniture, or other object. The child usually practices his first symbol many times and refines it considerably before he begins developing his second symbol. But there are exceptions to this; some children may work at refining two or more symbols at a time.

The most commonly selected second symbols are buildings. As the child practices and refines these he can differentiate between house, church, apartment building, and others. Study of the art of kindergarten children ages 4 to 6 shows that 56 percent of their drawings include humans and 36 percent include buildings. In descending order after that are mechanical objects 15 percent, animals 11 percent, trees 7 percent, furniture and toys 3 percent, and flowers 1 percent. These choices depend largely on the children's experiences with the objects and their interest in them. Most children, of course, also select other objects of particular interest to them, which are not on the list of especially popular symbols.

While the child is developing his symbols he still retains some characteristics of the manipulative stage. Often he gets carried away with the fun of using the material and proceeds to destroy his creations. He enjoys destroying his works as much as he enjoys making them in the first place. All teachers who allow their children to paint have seen this. A teacher may see a vigorous, attractive painting a child is working on, and then look a few moments later to see it all painted over with a dark color. The teacher may be dismayed, but the child has had fun.

The following drawing with accompanying chatter by Mark, age 4½, shows what happens. Notice the vacillation between the pronouns I and he, the eventual metamorphosis of the boy into a rabbit, and the final concern with it being "pretty" instead of being a recognizable object.

I'll draw me, how big I am.

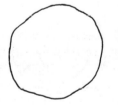

Mouth and eyes and nose.

Now lookit.

How bout arms?
Now lookit.

What does that look like
with a line here?

Now lookit.

Now lookit.
Ha ha, he's funny like that.

All this is my shirt
and this mask on him
is for Halloween.

See? *(What did that do?)* I
don't know.

There's his ears on here.

This is gonna be a rabbit.
A rabbit. Da, da, da, da, dom.

Look what I'm doing.
I can't do up here like that;
it has ears on here.

It's a rabbit and it's carrying
something in his mouth like that.

Now lookit. Round O on his head.
Isn't that pretty like that?

Jason, age 6½, starts out to draw himself, but the boy turns into an "it."

Jason says, "It can't sit down because of the box is in the way, and the box can't turn."

Here again is incomplete control of the symbol. It works better to name the object after it is drawn than to announce it beforehand. But these vestiges of the manipulative stage gradually are left behind as the child moves further into the representative stage and handles his symbols well.

When two or more symbols are put together in a composition and related in thought, a new phase begins—the phase of relating symbols to an environment. Two people together may be titled "Me and My Mother." From this point on, what we tend to think of as "pictures" can be produced. Children can make family groupings, pictures of themselves or others doing something, pictures of events in stories. This level usually has its beginnings in kindergarten and it develops greatly during primary grades.

Sometimes children make what is called "X-ray" pictures. In these they draw what they know is there, regardless of whether it can actually be seen from the viewer's perspective. Thus the contents of a pocket may show through the pants, chairs may show through people, and so forth. "Series" pictures show events in the order a child thinks of them, regardless of whether they are connected in time or space. "Fold-over" pictures result from the child's ingenuity in depicting difficult scenes. For instance, people seated around a table may be shown as radiating outward from the table. Adults viewing such a picture feel they need to fold the people up to sitting position to get a proper perspective.

In making pictures, children eventually add a "base-line" which is not the same as a horizon line. It will be the floor or ground upon which objects can stand. Later a skyline will be used, and it probably will not be until age 8 to 10 that the skyline and the baseline will eventually meet in a horizon line.

If something is important to a child he may make it larger. For instance, the mother may be larger than the house in his drawing. Color is often chosen emotionally, and the child will draw something in his favorite color rather than in its realistic color.

The representative stage of art, as we have seen, has two phases:

1. Emerging and developing symbols
2. Relating symbols to an environment

Children at kindergarten ages may be entering into the representative stage, but most will not be far advanced in it. The greatest development here will take place during primary years, but the foundations of interest and attitude and work habits are laid in the preschool and kindergarten years.

In summary, the early developmental sequence of children's art is as follows:

> Manipulative stage
>> Random manipulation
>> Controlled manipulation
>> Named manipulation

Representative stage
   Emerging and developing symbols
   Relating symbols to an environment
Kindergarten children will for the most part be moving from the manipulative stage into the representative stage. Those more experienced with art media will be well along in developing their symbols and some children will begin relating symbols in pictures. Children less experienced with art media will usually move rapidly through the manipulative phases and on into the representative stage. In other words, they will catch up with their peers. The point at which this rapid development slows to a more normal pace depends on the children's general mental development.

God, the Source and Goal of Art

Art expression is a universal phenomenon. It is found in all times, in all parts of the world, in all cultures, among all peoples. Social scientists do not profess to know what motivates people to art, but they acknowledge that it is normal for everyone to manipulate materials to bring order out of chaos. The young child makes mud pies and the adult arranges a room.

In the beginning God created the earth. It was without form, and from the shapeless mass God with His creative acts made a world that He called good. From the dust of the earth He formed man and breathed into him life. Man was made in the image of God.

Who can say what all might be included in that phrase, "image of God"? The first thing we read about God in the Bible is His great creative acts, and if man is in the image of that God certainly there is something of that creativity built into man from the beginning. Creativity that comes from God should do nothing less than praise God, and reflect the goodness and beauty and truth that are found in Him and His works.

Art educators who leave God out of their thinking

still know that people have an innate creativity which reaches out in numerous ways, including art expression. And without acknowledging God as the originator of creativity they often raise man to that position; thus art becomes a process of self-expression. It is not unusual to find this view in art education books. A major purpose of art in kindergartens, according to many of the books, is to help children find socially acceptable ways to express their feelings and emotions. These books state that feelings are neither good nor bad; they simply exist and they should be expressed.

This unbiblical view of good and evil within the child is the false base from which the "emotional-outlet" idea of art is derived. And the high view of self is the base for the "self-expression" idea. These uses for art are sometimes repeated in our Christian education books as well. No doubt this is often due to someone unthinkingly picking up phrases from education books and too glibly passing them on as being good education practice, but the sad fact is that the cult of the self has widely infiltrated Christian education writings and practices in our day.

Now, it is true that angry children may pound the clay or paint bold black strokes, or stab a brush onto a paper and say, "I'll kill you." It is also true that timid children may make tiny drawings of themselves, and happy children may make bright, airy paintings. But is this sort of thing the basis for art in our Christian education programs?

Christian education aims to produce the fruit of the Spirit, not to express the works of the flesh. Christian education is for learning about God—the truth and beauty that are found in Him. Christian education is to inspire worship and praise. Art can relate to these and other high aims of Christian education. Certainly beauty is a gift from God; and skill, ability and pleasure in producing it are also gifts from Him, as is the creativity found in every person. We should think of art as expressing truth and beauty, as praising God, as expressing joy and peace and goodness. Christian use of art is God-expression, not self-expression.

Of course, when a child does something he does it with his whole self. There is no separating of emotions, body, or mind. And we cannot separate these things in our teaching of art, or our use of art in Bible teaching. All elements will be there, and the self is inevitably going to be expressed. But the crucial question is, "Where should we place our emphasis?" Our philosophy shows in the purpose we have for using art, and the direction we take with it.

A humanistic philosophy sees self-expression as an end in itself. It is a "good" to strive for in art education. But a Christian view aims for the growth of Christlikeness in the child, and it sees artistic expression as one means of contributing to that growth. If art is an expression of the inner self, then Christian education must aim to produce a better self. But since there is no good in man, and a person's goodness comes only from God, we are led to the conclusion mentioned earlier, that good art is God-expression and not self-expression.

Christian teachers may not need to understand a great deal about philosophies of art education, but we do need to "beware," as Paul says in Colossians 2:8, that we be not spoiled through "philosophy and vain deceit," after the traditions of the world, and not after Christ. The self-expression emphasis in art is certainly one of these rudiments of the world that has invaded Christian education, and Paul's word "beware" is still the best advice concerning it.

Creativity Versus Directed Art

Some teachers are going to say, "But I'm not teaching art; I'm teaching Bible." These teachers may feel that coloring a picture or producing a directed, uncreative handwork item often helps to teach the lesson, and that these are justified because they teach Bible even though they may not teach art.

Here, then, is a dilemma. Are we interested primarily in developing art abilities of the child, or are we more interested in producing a recognizable take-home item that says something about the lesson? It is a complicated question with no easy answers. In fact, it probably has no answer at the present time that can be demonstrated convincingly. Lesson publishers are trying to provide some of both—a handwork sheet that will say something about the lesson when it arrives at home, but to which the child can add his creative touch. Certainly almost everyone agrees that there is no value in entirely uncreative work—the kind where children carry out directions and all produce identical items to hang in rows around the room.

Drawing or any art work is not learned by drilling on the physical skills; it comes from the mind. When Joni Eareckson became a quadriplegic she thought she would not be able to draw anymore. But a therapist told her the drawing skill was not in her hand; it was in her head. With this encouragement, she learned to hold a pen in her mouth and draw the pictures that were in her head. If your children draw ears too large, or if they leave out the trunk of a person and attach legs directly to the head, it is not drawing lessons they need so much as time for the mind to develop more, and opportunity for their powers of observation to be sharpened. One way to sharpen their observation and develop their thinking is through drawing—their way, not ours.

An experiment with 250 children of primary ages was set up to help determine the effects of dictatorial methods of teaching. All the children had been in a program of creative art, but at the time of the experiment 125 of them were given ten lessons of a restrictive or dictatorial nature, while the remaining 125 continued with their regular creative experiences. The restrictive art lessons consisted of copying drawings from the blackboard or mimeographed sheets, coloring or tracing drawings, following verbal directions to produce drawings, and cutting geometric forms such as a triangle and a square to make a house. In these ways they made pictures of such things as an apple, tree, flower, bird, or snowman.

On the eleventh day both groups were taken to a fire station and on their return to school were asked to make pictures of their experiences. The drawings and paintings of the "creative" group illustrated their observations and personal reactions and were successful in varying degrees, while 44 percent of the "restrictive" group failed to depict the fire station outing at all, but resorted to doing flowers, trees and other items in the manner which they had been taught in the previous ten days. Still others in this group regressed to the stage of manipulation of the art media, rather than performing at their usual higher stage—that of being able to produce symbols.

In another study 5000 children of kindergarten ages 4 to 6 were studied for a period of two years. Results of using adult designed models were much the same as in the primary level study. Some children who had formerly copied adult symbols were retarded in their own art progress for the full two years. If a child is given only one adult symbol, he may still make progress in devising his own symbols for other objects. But if he is given many symbols, there is little opportunity left for his own development in art. In such cases the children tended to become classroom problems because they had difficulty thinking for themselves.

If restrictive art lessons can have such devastating effect, we need to be careful about our use of art, even though we are not art teachers. We would not use poor grammar as a model for our children and excuse it by saying we are teaching Bible, not language. Likewise, we do not use what we consider poor music. In every other area we consider the development of children, and it should be the same in art. All children, of course, will not grow up to be artists, but all should experience art creatively.

The creative approach to art not only develops the aesthetic nature; it also does more for children's cognitive development. The children who made their own decisions about how to show the fire station trip and who solved the problems in carrying out their plans were more active mentally and were active on a higher mental level than if the teacher had given them a fire truck to color, or had drawn a model station for them to copy.

Creative art does not mean that the teacher gives no guidance and the children do whatever they want. Art teaching takes stimulation—such as the fire station trip—and motivation and guidance when needed. The trick is to know when to help a child and when to let him solve his own problems.

Perhaps the reason some teachers do not use the more creative approach is that they fear they are not teaching Bible truths or facts unless the product of the children's work shows something about the Bible. It seems safer to give the child a sheep to color. The fallacy here may be that we have come to expect too much of handwork. If children are bent over a table and are busy with paper and pencil or crayon, it looks like school and it seems like "learning" to us, whereas if they are active and noisy it looks like play and wasted time. But children at a certain stage of development can actually be learning more about sheep by crawling around on the floor pretending to eat grass, and being herded into a fold and other game-like or pretend activities. When sheep are firmly in their minds, and when they have reached the stage of development where they can draw symbols which stand for sheep, then the products of their art work are more likely to satisfy teachers who want something recognizable in children's art.

It might be better if we relied less on art or handwork and made more use of games, rhymes, sound stories, conversation, pretend activities and other kinds of learning. Many lessons can be planned with a rich variety of activities and never use handwork at all. Sometimes in published lesson sheets for children the emphasis is on something other than handwork. The sheet may fold into a booklet to learn to read, or it may be a talk-about sheet where the children name things and tell what is happening.

When we do use art it would be better to lean toward creative uses rather than the restrictive, directed uses. Worship use for art is a largely unexplored area. Children could enjoy the beautiful colors God made. They could express joy in using the hands God gave them. One four-year-old was painting with blue when the teacher said quietly, "God made blue." "He did?" the child exclaimed with surprise in his voice, and he painted his blue with new vigor—God's blue. After an experience like that no teacher in her right mind would want to pull the child's thinking down to the level needed to complete a directed painting lesson—even with blue.

Art as Learning and Growing

Often we try to put art activities into a neat little category of their own. We say art or handwork is the "doing" part of the lesson. Or we say it is the expression part; after the children have learned the lesson, they are to "express" what they have learned. Or we even say it is the application of the lesson.

The expression idea sometimes comes close to what happens, but the other duties we have assigned to art are quite unrealistic. Consider, for instance, a lesson on obeying parents. The children can have a Bible story about Joseph obeying his father and going to look for his brothers. They can play the story and "be" Joseph, looking and looking even when it is a long way, and finding the brothers at last, as father said to do. They can sing a song about obeying; do an action rhyme; learn the Bible verse, "Children obey your parents"; play a game that reinforces the meaning of *obey*. They can talk about obeying their own parents, and make plans for obeying in specific instances, such as going to bed when asked, or taking out the garbage or performing another specific chore. They can roleplay some of these situations.

Now, the real lesson application comes in the homes later where the children show whether the lesson has made any difference in their cheerful willingness to obey. The "doing," as nearly as it can be accomplished in a lesson hour, comes in the roleplaying, the game, the conversation, and the thinking that accompanies these and other lesson activities. If the children are given a picture of Joseph to color or a maze to "help find the brothers," or similar lesson sheet it will be much less effective than most of the other lesson activities. It's not at all close to doing the lesson, and it certainly is not applying the lesson.

A better art activity in such a lesson would be for the children to draw pictures of themselves obeying their parents. The thinking that goes into such an activity would help to promote the lesson aim. Good conversation and roleplay should precede, to help stimulate the children's thinking, and children should use their own choice of what to do in their pictures. This assignment, of course, will only work with children who have reached the representational stage in their drawing ability.

The example above is from one of the few lessons that can have a clear-cut behavior-type aim. When the children are learning that God is great, that He made all things, that Jesus is God's Son and other great themes of

Scripture such an aim is not possible. In these lessons the expressional idea of art may fit better.

But there is no simple formula of 1) learn first, 2) express next. Children and teacher can admire together some flowers God made. Then the children can paint flowers or make flowers from paper and other materials. In the process of their work or after their work they will look again at the real flowers with a new awareness. The art activity, in other words, is a learning experience; it sharpens the children's powers of observation and heightens their appreciation of beauty, color, form, complexity. Looking at the flowers afterward can become an experience of worship of the God who made them. So we could describe the art activity as learning and the worship or new appreciation as the expression which follows.

This more complex view shows that art cannot be neatly categorized as the "expression" part of the lesson or the "doing" part of the lesson. Art is simultaneously learning and expression, and it is much more besides.

God created wondrous beauties for man to enjoy, and He created man with an aesthetic side to his nature so he can enjoy them. One of man's first jobs was to dress the garden and keep it. God's plan for the tabernacle included elaborate art work, for which He gave men the necessary skills. Some of the greatest art in the history of the world is that which was done to the glory of God.

Children grow aesthetically, just as they grow physically, mentally and every other way. If we don't block the road too much, this will happen. In other words, we can allow art simply for art's sake or for aesthetic growth. We don't always need an academic reason (Draw what you learned in the story today), or a psychological reason (He's expressing his hostility in this painting), or any other reason to justify art.

We give opportunities for children to grow in their language, their muscular coordination, their singing, and numerous other ways. We can let them grow in art as well.

Kindergarten children are not too young to profit from great Christian art, or even the not-so-great—the pictures in their Sunday school papers and other materials. They can notice how the artist uses bright colors to make something cheerful, or somber colors to make a stormy sky. They can look at contrasting textures. A landscape done in pointillism will start many children experimenting themselves with the dabbing brush stroke.

Children's diet should not be only sweetness and light. Sometimes people in Bible story pictures are angry. Look at their faces. How does the artist make them look angry? Does anything else about their bodies look angry too? Look at a picture of Jesus on the cross. Talk about pain, sorrow, love.

When a particular picture "catches on" with your children, display it for a time prominently. Try placing it in the center of a bulletin board and place around it your children's paintings or drawings that seem to be motivated by its color or style or content.

What do you say when you look at a child's painting? Teachers and parents used to say, "What is it?" The child may not have made anything in particular. Indeed, he may not yet be capable of doing so. But to please the adult he responded to this question with some kind of name for his picture. Then the adult tried to hide his astonishment and remarked, "Oh, I see. It does look like that." The next time the child began a painting he was restricted by that experience. He now believed he had to produce something recognizable to an adult.

Later, teachers began instructing parents to say, "Tell me about it." This is more open ended, but it still requires the child to put into words what he has chosen to put in paint. When people admire a sunset, a rainbow or a tree, some may want to tell everyone around them how beautiful it is, while others may feel unable to express what they see and feel. The poet might use words and the painter, his paints. And once the painter has made his statement, who expects him to do it better in words?

When your little painter holds up his painting for your comment, you must be very careful. Your manner cannot suggest to him that you're saying what you think you're supposed to say. You can't use a stock remark such as "It's beautiful" or "I like it"—at least not more than once. You have to look at the picture long enough to make some sincere and meaningful remarks about it. If the symbols are recognizable you can comment about the content of the picture. If it seems only scribbles to you, find something about the colors or shapes or line motions or other features to comment on. At this, many children will respond with profuse explanations of their own about their pictures. And even those who say nothing will still gain an increased awareness from your comments.

How do you help a child who says, "I can't make a donkey"? You help the child to help himself. Remember that the skill in making a donkey is in the head and not in the hand, as Joni Eareckson learned. So you help the child get a donkey in his head. "Let's see, a donkey. Will the donkey have a big body or a little body? Can he hear? What kind of ears will he have? Short ones or long ones? Shall we look again at the picture in our storybook?" Looking at pictures or at real objects is not to use them as models, but to help the child gain more impressions from which he forms his own meaning and inner image.

Do you need to help children with ideas? Yes. Part of your job as teacher is to help stimulate new ideas. Public school children visit the farm or fire station or airport to gain new experiences. Then they make drawings, which are both expression and further learning, as explained earlier. As Bible teacher you may be more limited in the matter of field trips, but there are some possibilities. You can go to see the baptistry and other parts of your church. You can look at your church from outside. You can go look at trees, birds, flowers and other things God made. You may be able to see sheep. You can see houses or apartment buildings where families live.

Next to real experiences are the vicarious experiences of pictures and stories. Help the children to experience these as fully as possible—by listening, talking, playing the stories, and perhaps having them in song or action rhyme form. After thorough teaching, some of the children's new learning is bound to come out in their art, just as it does in their speech and other actions. Your children will grow in art expression and in aesthetic awareness and appreciation.

READING CHECK

1. All children pass through the manipulative stage before reaching the representative stage.　　　　　　T　F

2. You can speed children's art development by teaching techniques for drawing people, trees and other items.　T　F

3. You can best help children draw particular items by helping them observe and learn about the items.　　T　F

4. Children develop some individual symbols first, and later relate these to each other in "pictures."　　　　T　F

5. Kindergarten children are usually well advanced into making pictures.　　　　　　　　　　　　　　　T　F

6. Art masterpieces are inappropriate for kindergarten children to study.　　　　　　　　　　　　　　T　F

7. Lesson-related handwork is one of the best ways for children to apply what they learn in a lesson.　　　T　F

Answers: 1—T, 2—F, 3—T, 4—T, 5—F, 6—F, 7—F

6 Music and Rhymes

- *Singing at Kindergarten Ages*
- *How to Teach a Song*
- *Carrying a Tune*
- *Songs for Kindergartners*
- *Singing Games*
- *Rhythm Instruments*
- *Rhythm and Rhymes*

Singing at Kindergarten Ages

Singing is one of the few abilities which pay to teach early. On most other matters we are still debating. For instance, opinions are divided about early reading. Does it really give children a head start, or does it just take a lot of time learning something which could be learned more easily and rapidly at a later age? With other kinds of learning, there are people who want to push more and more advanced concepts down to a lower and lower age, and there are people who object that this confuses children's minds with bits of knowledge they cannot integrate and handle properly.

But with singing, it has long been known that an early start is a head start that lasts. That is, later learning can never quite make up for missed learning at an earlier age. And, fortunately, the techniques for teaching singing at kindergarten level are quite simple and practically any teacher can learn to do it. Mostly, children need exposure to music of all kinds, but particularly singing, and they need opportunities themselves to sing.

TEACHING KINDERGARTNERS

It is helpful to understand how singing is produced. We know about voluntary muscles and involuntary muscles; a voluntary muscle in the arm will do what we direct it to do, and the involuntary heart muscle does its work without any orders from us. Now, the muscles of the vocal cords are somewhere between these two. We might say they operate on indirect orders. Those orders depend on mentally hearing the sound we wish to produce.

Right here is where most kindergarten musical training lies—giving opportunity to hear, and practice in reproducing singing sounds. One of the best ways to do this is to use simple songs with considerable repetition. Fortunately we have plenty of good, Biblical songs available for this purpose. These songs should generally be pitched within the range of Middle C up to A.

Song time is for enjoying the beauty of music and the pleasure in producing it. It is for praising God with singing, or praying to Him in song. It is for enjoying in musical form a variety of content—Bible verses and stories, behavior maxims (Oh, be careful little eyes what you see), nature poems, and fun movements. One thing song time is not, is a pep rally. Children should never be urged to sing loudly. The shouting that sometimes makes song leaders feel successful strains young vocal cords and teaches children improper ways to produce a singing tone.

Since hearing a tone is essential to producing the tone, children need opportunities to listen. When you teach new songs you can sing them to the children and let them listen. And you don't need to rush them from listening to singing. If you sing a song once and then say, "Now you sing it with me this time," that may be too soon for many of your children. The amount of listening needed will of course vary according to the difficulty of the song and the abilities of the children. Listening and singing can be alternated in the learning of a song. That is, after the children have tried singing it you can have them listen again to you, and then try singing it again.

How to Teach a Song

Teaching a song may proceed like this. Let's consider teaching the chorus of "Oh, How I Love Jesus." The words are these.

> Oh, how I love Jesus,
> Oh, how I love Jesus,
> Oh, how I love Jesus
> Because He first loved me.

You can begin the teaching by singing the song once or twice for the children. This might be done immediately before the children are to sing it, or it might be in an earlier part of the class session, such as in a story where you show how a little child sang the song. After the children have heard the song you could call their attention to the last line, perhaps by asking why you love Jesus. They can say the answer together—"Because He first loved me." Then you could sing the answer and have them sing it after you. Then tell the children to listen to you sing the whole song, and to join you on that line. This technique gets children to listen with more concentration than otherwise, and they will be learning the whole song and not just the line they sing. You might do the song once or several times in this manner, with the children joining on the last line. And, finally, they could join you on the whole song.

You can call attention to other details, as needed by your group. For instance, you could emphasize that they sing "Oh, how I love Jesus" three times, by having them put up their fingers—one, two, three—as you sing the three lines. You can show how the tones go higher and lower by raising and lowering your hand. Here, for instance, is the highest part, at the end of line 2.

Je - su - us

All songs need not be taught in exactly the same way. With more difficult songs you may sing them for the children during several class sessions so they hear it many times before you begin asking them to sing it. With very simple songs you need not take time to have the children first sing one part as in the example above, but they can sing the whole song with you after having opportunity to hear it.

In general, it is best to stick with the "whole" method. That is, the song is usually sung as a whole, and not learned phrase by phrase. Notice in the example given, that even when the children sang only the last line the teacher sang the rest so that the song remained whole, except for the one time when the children tried out their line first. This sort of "part" work should be used only occasionally. It should not be used as the main teaching method wherein the children learn one phrase after another until the whole song is put together.

Accompaniment is not essential for kindergarten singing; teacher and children can just sing together with no accompaniment. If there is a piano in the room it is instructive to hit the first note of the song and have everyone listen and try to start on the same note. Or use a pitch pipe for this.

For variety and to help acquaint children with the use of instruments, accompaniments may be used on some songs. If you can play even very simply on a piano and if your classroom has one, the children will enjoy it if you use the piano on certain songs you have learned. Children can follow better a simple, uncluttered accompaniment. If you know three or four chords on a guitar you could play certain other songs on it. An autoharp is good to use, too. This small instrument is held on the lap and takes practically no time to learn and no advanced musical education is needed.

Carrying a Tune

Many kindergarten children do not match all the tones accurately. That is, they do not "carry a tune" as our common phrase expresses it. For this reason kindergarten teachers often invent games to provide practice on this. Question and answer games are common. The teacher may sing, "Where is Ji-ill?" and she is to answer on the same tones, "I am he-ere." Such games can often be made to fit Bible stories. When angels sing, "Holy, holy, holy," the teacher can sing it and have the children listen and match the tune. Various children may make up tunes, too, for the others to match. Or just sing the one word "Holy" on one tone and let individual children match the tone. The sheep can bleat "Baa" on a high tone and the lion can "Roar" on a low tone.

Such games do help children to concentrate on listening and hearing accurately the various tones. But they should be used only as long as they are games. They should not degenerate to merely drill, since with music the emotional aspect is highly important. Children should learn above all else to love music and enjoy it. If a singer performs a song with good technical mastery, but without love of the song, a most important ingredient is missing.

Sometimes when children do not carry the tune it is simply that they do not know the song well enough. One teacher remembers singing "Jesus Loves Me" around his home when he was five years old and only half knew the song. He repeated the phrase "Yes, Jesus loves me" too many times and on tunes he was making up as he went along. This was his way of enjoying the song even though he could not remember how many times to repeat the phrase. An older sister chided the boy, saying, "You don't know how to carry a tune." The five-year-old tried to argue that he was making up his own tune, but the incident was a hurt he carried for many years and it made him afraid to sing in the presence of others.

Making up tunes is an important aspect of musical education. Spontaneous singing at opportune times in a classroom shows music as integrated with life. A teacher who feels comfortable with this approach can sing a one-line song about Harry's shiny, brown shoes, or about the bright red crayon, or the fish that swims round and round. It is a special delight to this kind of teacher when children pick up this habit too. When this happens, the teacher ought to recognize the song but be careful not to embarrass the child who made it.

Songs for Kindergartners

Children's music should not be entirely apart from the music they will enjoy when they are older. It is wise to choose many of their songs from our common heritage of beloved Christian songs. Sometimes a simple change of a word or two will make songs have more meaning for young children. Instead of "I am bound for the promised land," sing "I am going to the promised land." This is a straightforward, simple statement that children can easily understand. Notice, too, how the chorus of this song has a repetitious pattern that is an earmark of good, easy-to-learn songs for children.

> I am going to the promised land,
> I am going to the promised land.
> Oh, who will come and go with me?
> I am going to the promised land.

Change "O Beulah land" to "O Heaven land." In "Praise Him . . . all ye little children," sing "all *you* little children." Instead of "There is a green hill far away without a city wall," make the meaning clear by singing *"outside* a city wall."

Sing the choruses of "What a Wonderful Savior," "Trust and Obey," "Jesus Loves Even Me" and "Battle Hymn of the Republic." Some hymns should be sung in their entirety, as the traditional children's song, "Away in a Manger." Try "For the Beauty of the Earth," and "I Think When I Read That Sweet Story." Try "Where He Leads Me" and "Silent Night."

Here are some words to "Just As I Am" which were written in the nineteenth century by Marianne

Farmingham. They are older than the words commonly found in today's hymn books, and more suitable for young children. There is nothing here nearly as obscure as, "waiting not to rid my soul of one dark blot." Instead of "Lamb of God" this says simply, "Jesus Christ."

> Just as I am, Thine own to be,
> Friend of the young, who lovest me,
> To consecrate myself to Thee,
> O Jesus Christ I come, I come.

Folk tunes are another part of our common musical heritage. These have proved by their long history to have an eminently singable quality, and when we put Christian words to them they will live long in our children's memories. Most of these tunes extend for at least an octave, and thus have a wider range than the six notes recommended for young children's voices. Sometimes this problem can be skirted by changing a note or two, as is commonly done anyway in the history of folk singing. But often this is not necessary. An extra high note may be touched lightly only once during the song. Also, the singable quality of these tunes helps children to hear them and learn them more easily than some of our modern tunes.

"Twinkle, Twinkle, Little Star" is sung to a French folk tune. We can use Jane Taylor's famous words with one slight change and have a biblical song that children love.

> Twinkle, twinkle, little star,
> God has made you what you are
> Up above the world so high,
> Like a diamond in the sky.
> Twinkle, twinkle, little star,
> God has made you what you are.

Some folk songs and spirituals had a biblical base originally and can be used as they are. Here are two examples.

ALL NIGHT, ALL DAY

WHO BUILT THE ARK?

Some folk tunes suit themselves to simple, repetitious words that children learn in no time at all. Here are two examples of such tunes. In the first one children may help make up words for the last line, according to the Bible stories they know.

SEA OF GALILEE

Ruth Beechick   Folk

At the Sea of Ga - li - lee. At the Sea of Ga - li - lee.

At the Sea of Ga - li - lee
1. Je - sus called four fish - er - men.
2. Je - sus stilled the wind and waves.
3. Je - sus walked on wa - ter.

4. Peter walked on water.
5. Jesus said, "Let down your nets."
6. Jesus cooked some fish and bread.

7. Jesus said, "Come follow me."
8. Jesus taught the people.
(Children may make up additional stanzas.)

I WILL LOVE THE BIBLE

Chords names are for use with autoharp.

Some groups of children are able to learn more complex sets of words. Many children love the space ideas in this song, which is also set to a folk tune.

GOD'S TEMPLE

Ruth Beechick

II Chronicles 6:18

Folk

The sky is stretched a - bove the world And reach - es 'round it all.

But sky a - lone is not God's home: The sky is much too small.

The out - er space goes on and on A - way be - yond it all

But out - er space is not God's home: The space is much too small.

But God wants to live in me. He wants to live in me.

TEACHING KINDERGARTNERS

In addition to the hymns, choruses, and folk tunes already mentioned, there are other kinds of songs, written especially for children. These include well-known Bible story songs, such as "Only a Boy Named David," "The Wise Man and the Foolish Man," and "Zacchaeus." There are prayer songs, and there are Bible verse songs—Scripture verses set to music.

With such a wide variety of music we should be able to give our children a good start musically. Some teachers may need to expand their own musical horizons along with their children's. There is much good music to select from these days, and this should be a joy to both the teacher and the children.

Singing Games

Singing games have many values for children. It is a fortunate class which has a teacher who enjoys music and games with them. Shy children are often helped in this way to participate as a part of a group. Children can get needed large-muscle activity—also small-muscle activity. Games can provide a change of pace in the class period and set the stage for quieter activities to follow. And there is teaching value in the repetition of words and actions related to familiar Bible stories. It is a form of learning by doing.

Singing games build upon natural interests of children. And they give children opportunity to use their energy. Music experiences are enriching to the child both now and for his future.

It is good to build a repertoire of games that your children know well and can do at appropriate times in your class sessions with them—not too many games at the first, just a few which the children will enjoy repeating over and over. Then you can occasionally add a new one to their active repertoire.

To teach a game, do not explain everything to the children at once. Just get them in starting position and

begin. The children can follow you in words and actions until they catch on to the game themselves.

Children will enjoy the games more if they can actually make circles and other game formations to do them. But if your circumstances require it, many of the games can be modified to use classroom seating arrangement.

Children will vary in their abilities to keep time with the music, to imitate actions, and to remember game sequences. You can help individual children to participate on their own levels and not make it hard for children who cannot do as well as others. You can also encourage the children's creative ideas and not insist upon strict conformity. There is no need to insist that every child participate. If one is unwilling to do so, value his individuality and let him wait until he is ready to join the group in these activities.

Enjoyment of singing games is contagious. It begins with the teacher and spreads to the children.

The beginning of singing games is the motion song. Here is the action song which the children in the opening chapter of this book were using, although they had made their own arrangement with rhythm instruments instead of using the motions given here.

ABRAHAM

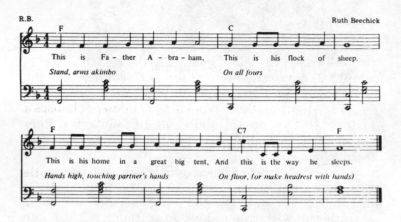

Here is a simple game which needs no particular game formation, although a circle can be used if desired. The song may first be sung about Adam or Samuel or other Bible person from a lesson. Use the tune, "Mary Had a Little Lamb."

> God gave Adam work to do,
> Work to do, work to do.
> God gave Adam work to do;
> He did it very well.

Choose a volunteer to come to the front. All the children sing about her. "God gave Alice work to do . . . . She does it very well." Either during the singing or afterward, Alice pantomimes her work—setting the table, sweeping the floor, or other chore. The children guess. Then a new worker is chosen and the children sing again.

Here is a Farmer-in-the-Dell type game sung to that tune. To start, one child is in the center. He names any animal he wishes to, for instance, bear. Then all the children sing.

God made the bear,
God made the bear,
Back when the world was new
God made the bear.

While the verse is being sung, the center child walks about and chooses a bear from the circle. Bear goes to the center and joins the first child. After the stanza Bear names a new animal. Everyone sings and Bear chooses a child to be that animal and come to the center. Play continues until all children are in the center and there is no circle left.

If your group of children is not yet able to handle circle formations you can simply have Bear and the other animals come to the front and stand by you. This adaptation can also be used in cases where the room is not large enough to accommodate a circle game. Never be afraid to adapt a game that you find in a book. There really are no mandatory, "official" ways to do them.

Another familiar game uses the London Bridge idea. Two children form a bridge by joining hands up high. The other children file under the bridge and all sing.

Heaven is a happy place,
Happy place, happy place,
Heaven is a happy place,
Hallelujah.

On "Hallelujah" one child is caught and he trades places with a child who forms the bridge.

Many children need guidance, as they trade places in this game or as they choose animals in the previous game. The total picture of the game and its sequence do not become clear to them until the game has been done many times. This kind of learning is one of the values of games.

Here is a longer, more complicated sequence which plays out a whole Bible story. It can be sung either to the tune of "Mary Had a Little Lamb" or "Mulberry Bush."

RACHEL AND JACOB

Meredith Goodrich

Tune: Mary Had A Little Lamb

1. Ra-chel was a shep-herd girl, shep-herd girl, shep-herd girl.
(One girl is Rachel and stands in front.)

Ra-chel was a shep-herd girl; she watched her fath-ers sheep 2.And

2. And everywhere that Rachel went,
   Rachel went, Rachel went,
   Everywhere that Rachel went
   The sheep were sure to go.

   Rachel walks round and round the children who are singing.

3. They followed to the well one day,
   Well one day, well one day,
   They followed to the well one day,
   Which was the thing to do.

   Rachel walks to the "well" (two chairs facing each other).

4. There was Jacob at the well,
   At the well, at the well,
   There was Jacob at the well.
   He watered Rachel's sheep.

   A boy (Jacob) stands on other side of the well.

5. Jacob loved her very much,
   Very much, very much,
   Jacob loved her very much
   And she became his wife.

   Jacob and Rachel each go touch another child who will be the next Jacob and Rachel.

It is not as difficult as it may look to create such songs and games to go with any particular Bible lesson. Notice in the song above how each stanza is made from only two lines, and they are unrhymed. Using this pattern with your own Bible lesson you might come up with this.

> Noah build a great, big boat . . .
> Out of gopher wood.

With a few more stanzas about the animals and family getting inside, the rain coming, and so forth, you can put the whole story into song form. Add an action for each stanza and, Presto, you have a game. Other tunes which take this two-line, non-rhyming arrangement of words are "Muffin Man" and "London Bridge." "Round the Village," "Skip to My Lou," and "Ten Little Indians" take a slightly different arrangement of words, but still only two lines. If you get interested in this kind of invention you will find many other possibilities with familiar tunes or with your own tunes.

Rhythm Instruments

Some years ago kindergarten rhythm bands were popular. They were supposed to be good for musical and rhythmical training and for training in cooperation— following directions and working together in a group. These bands are not used widely now, because we no longer value such conformity. We value, instead, individual thinking and creativity.

Today kindergarten children are more likely to be asked to make their own arrangements. They may listen to a piece of music, decide which instrument to use and when to play it. The arrangement will never be static; different children will play it differently, the same child will do it differently on a new occasion, and it is seldom memorized for display to parents.

Rhythm training helps children to a greater awareness in both music and speech. Even though we only slip in a bit of rhythm teaching now and then it will be valuable. Children will see the songs, words, and stories in a new dimension, and their lives will be enriched.

A simple activity is to clap the rhythm of your children's names—Tif-fa-ny, Ja-son, Bill. You can clap a child's name and have him clap it back to you. The whole class can clap it together. Bring two or three children to the front and clap one of the names. Have the class listen closely and see if they can tell you whose name you clapped. Children will enjoy making up tunes for their names, too. They can sing the tunes and try to find them on the piano or bells.

Use these same procedures in teaching some of the Bible words you want your children to become familiar with—Jerusalem, Bethlehem, Sea of Galilee, obey, believe.

Instruments can be used occasionally with singing. One or two children can play drums or sticks or bells or something else, while the rest sing. Since more children will want turns you will have to sing the song several times. Sometimes everyone may play at once. In a lesson about David you could make harps (rubber bands stretched around a box) and all play together as you sing a song David might have sung.

Sometimes use instruments with rhymes. A child could play two tone bells alternately while the group recites a rhyme. Keeping step with the rhyme this way adds an interesting dimension to it.

Sometimes use instruments to add sound effects to stories. A way to do this is explained in the chapter, "About Stories."

Books on rhythm instruments will describe numerous kinds you can make inexpensively. Here, we will suggest just a few. Some of these are simple enough that the children could help make them as a class activity.

cymbals

Pot covers make good cymbals.
Heavier lids are better than thin
aluminum ones. Strike two lids
together, or strike one lid with a stick
or wooden spoon. Second-hand
stores, or garage sales may be good
sources of pot covers.

drums

Use oatmeal boxes with or without
lids. Beat with knuckles, or
with stick or wooden spoon. Try
other kinds of boxes too.
Decorate as desired and attach a
yarn neck strap if you wish.

127

flutes

Blow just right across the top of a
bottle for a beautiful flute
sound. Smaller bottles make higher
notes. This is a challenge
for kindergartners. Some can do
it and some have yet to learn.

harps

Use open boxes and stretch rubber
bands of different sizes around
them.

shakers

Place beans, peas, pebbles, or other loose material in pill bottles or small boxes. Tape boxes shut and decorate as desired. Play by shaking.

sticks

Use dowel lengths or make country-style sticks by splitting a length of hardwood. File and sand until smooth. Plain sticks are played by hitting. To make sticks for rubbing, wrap and tack sandpaper onto a pair of sticks or notch one of each pair. Notches can be made by lathes or by hand by making coping saw cuts and chiseling out the wood between some of the cuts.

tone jars

Use small jars such as baby food jars. Tune by filling with various amounts of water. Children practice arranging the jars from low to high. They may make up tunes of their own.

trumpets

Use the cardboard tube from waxed paper or paper toweling. Place waxed paper on one end with a rubber band. Poke a hole in the tube near this end. Play by humming or "Ta-taing" into the other end.

triangles

Many common objects can make
satisfactory triangle sounds. Look
around your basement or garage for
possibilities. Use nails, horseshoes,
forks, coat hangers, or pieces of
rods or tubing made of brass, steel, or
iron. Suspend the "triangle" by a
string and play by striking
with another fork, nail, rod, or whatever
is used.

wood blocks

Attach handles to blocks of wood.
Knock together for sound. A
substitute for this sound can be made
by knocking together the bowls
of two wooden spoons.

131

Rhythm and Rhymes

Rhythm is an aid to memory. To recite a Bible story in rhythmic form, or to include rhythm in memory verse practice, adds another dimension that impresses the mind more indelibly than otherwise. Rhyme and other alliterative aspects of verse have this effect too.

A pastor who spent three years in solitary confinement in a communist prison preached himself a sermon each day in order to keep his mind sound. Then, to remember the sermons, he organized his main points in verse form. After his freedom he was able to recall the verses and through them to reconstruct more than three hundred of the sermons.

People who have grown up with only a small amount of Sunday school experience in their early years may end up knowing only a few things that were in rhyme form. All else may be forgotten. Prisoners of war and others in the hard places of life sometimes recall first, "Jesus Loves Me." If they learned other rhymes or songs as children they piece together other bits of Bible knowledge.

All of us who learned nursery rhymes still remember "Little Bo Peep" or "Little Boy Blue." The rhymes and rhythms helped us to remember so long. Another memory aid was the many repetitions that parents, teachers and children tend to give to rhymes.

Bible rhymes are good teaching for the children's immediate learning, and they may be even more valuable far down the years. Here are several ways to use them.

Action Rhymes. We use the term "action rhymes" because this is more inclusive than fingerplays. These rhymes often involve movements of arms and body, as well as fingers.

Some lesson books or rhyme books advise that the rhymes are not for the children to learn; the children are to follow along with the motions while the teacher recites or reads the rhyme. The reason for this advice is that the words are complicated; there are too many of them for the children to learn well. Such rhymes, no doubt, have a use in adding variety to a lesson, but they fall short of the powerful learning that rhymes can achieve.

A rhyme for the children to learn has a pattern that is easy to catch on to and easy to remember. Here are two examples of such rhymes.

JUST A LITTLE OIL

JUST a little OIL	*(Cup one hand.)*
And JUST a little FLOUR—	*(Cup other hand.)*
The LAdy had eNOUGH	*(Invert one cup on other cup*
For a LITtle loaf of BREAD.	*to form loaf.)*

"PLEASE use your OIL	*(Cup.)*
And PLEASE use your FLOUR	*(Cup.)*
To MAKE a loaf for ME,"	*(Loaf.)*
ELIjah SAID.	

The LAdy shared her OIL	*(Cup.)*
And the LAdy shared her FLOUR.	*(Cup.)*
Then GOD gave her MORE	
And she ALways had BREAD.	*(Loaf.)*

THE LEPERS

HOW many LEPERS did JEsus MEET?
ONE, two, THREE, four, FIVE —
SIX, seven, EIGHT, nine, TEN.
HOW many LEPERS did JEsus HEAL?
ONE, two, THREE, four, FIVE —
SIX, seven, EIGHT, nine, TEN.
HOW many LEPERS came BACK and said THANKS?
ONE!
    (Raise one finger on each count.)

A good rule of thumb for measuring the difficulty of such rhymes is this: If an adult can remember the words after hearing the rhyme only once or twice, then it is about right for kindergartners. It may take the children more repetitions than that to learn the rhyme well, but they will be able to learn it.

The Pease Porridge motions are a fun challenge for kindergartners. It will take them longer to learn the motions than the words to this version of "Elijah Went Up." To go with more Bible lessons you may substitute the names Jesus, Enoch, John, or "the ladder." The motions, remember, are these.

1. Clap hands on knees.
2. Clap hands together.
3. Clap partner's hands.

1	2	3
ELIJAH	WENT	UP,
UP	TO	HEAVEN.
WHEN I	GO	UP
I'LL GO	TO	HEAVEN.

Along with your repertoire of songs, you should have several good rhymes ready at hand, too. They can be repeated just as songs are. This is a good way to achieve repetition and review of past Bible lessons.

Choral Speaking. Choral speaking is an ancient form of worship. At Mount Ebal and Mount Gerizim in Joshua's time, all the people stood on either side responding "Amen" as the blessings and the cursings in the law were read. Perhaps, as some say, those on Mount Gerizim said amen to the blessings and those on Mount Ebal said amen to the cursings. This giant outdoor antiphonal reading must have remained long in the memories of the little children present.

Even earlier, when the nation had just crossed the Red Sea, Moses and the men sang, "I will sing to the Lord; he hath triumphed gloriously. The horse and his rider hath he thrown into the sea." Even in English it sounds like a song. Miriam and the women took timbrels and answered them, "Sing ye to the Lord; he hath triumphed gloriously. The horse and his rider hath he thrown into the sea." For many days after that joyous occasion the little girls probably borrowed their mothers' timbrels, donned some dress-up clothes, and danced about the camp singing, "The horse and his rider hath he thrown into the sea." They may even have talked some boys into joining the play. One can almost hear them say, "You go over there. You're 'sposed to sing it first and we're 'sposed to answer you."

This antiphonal singing and speaking is still effective today. Choral readings can modify the antiphonal element and use any kind of variation that best fits the piece. Here is an example, taken from some thoughts in Job 38.

GOD CAN

TEACHER:	CAN you MAKE the MORNing COME?
CHILDREN:	I can't MAKE the MORNing COME.
TEACHER:	CAN you MAKE the SEA to STAY?
CHILDREN:	I can't MAKE the SEA to STAY.
TEACHER:	CAN you MOVE the STARS aROUND?
CHILDREN:	I can't MOVE the STARS aROUND.
TEACHER:	CAN you MAKE the WIND oBEY?
CHILDREN:	I can't MAKE the WIND oBEY.
ALL:	GOD can MAKE the MORNing COME.
	GOD can MAKE the SEA to STAY.
	GOD can MOVE the STARS aROUND.
	GOD can MAKE the WIND oBEY.

The method of teaching choral readings will vary from piece to piece, depending on how complicated the children's parts are. In general, use the "whole" method as much as possible. That is, give as brief preliminary instructions as you can and then proceed through the whole reading, helping children where necessary. Repeat the whole reading one or more additional times to learn it better. Once a reading is learned, remember to use it often, just as you do with songs.

Clapping Stories. The main idea in clapping stories is that you say a line and the children repeat it after you; then you say the next line and the children repeat it; and so forth, through all the lines. The whole time, a clapping rhythm is maintained, alternating with hands clapped together and hands clapped on laps.

Here are two examples of clapping stories. The accented (capitalized) words receive one clap and the unaccented words or spaces receive the alternate clap. It really doesn't matter which beat is the hand clap and which is the lap clap.

GIVING

	1		2		3	4
The	RICH	men	CAME	with	FAT	gold COINS.
The	WID —	ow	CAME	with	TWO	small PEN-nies.
	CLANK,	clank,	CLANK	went	FAT	gold COINS.
	PLINK,		PLINK	went	TWO	small PEN-nies.
	JE —	sus	SAID	those	RICH	men GAVE
A	LIT —	tle	PART	of	ALL	their MONEY.
The	WID —	ow	GAVE	much	MORE	than THEY.
For	SHE	has	GIV —	en	ALL	her MONEY.

JESUS MADE PEOPLE WELL

1		2		3		4
There WAS	a	MAN	who	COULD	not	SEE
Till JE —	sus	MADE	his	EYES	to	SEE,
AND	a	MAN	who	COULD	not	TALK
Till JE —	sus	MADE	his	TONGUE	to	TALK,
AND	a	MAN	who	COULD	not	HEAR
Till JE —	sus	MADE	his	EARS	to	HEAR,
AND	a	MAN	who	COULD	not	WALK
Till JE —	sus	MADE	his	LEGS	to	WALK.

Clapping stories, like the Pease Porridge motions, are not easy for the children to do well the first time you introduce them. These take a little work, but it is the challenging kind of work your children will love. Just do not discourage them by criticizing. Work on a story for several weeks, notice the improvement and tell the children how well they are doing.

If your group has extraordinary difficulty with the rhythm, try these lead-up systems. When they can do system 1 well, proceed to system 2. When they do that well, then move on to the lap-hand alternate clapping that is so fun to do with these stories.

1. Say each line in good rhythm, strongly emphasizing the accented syllables. The children say each line after you.

2. Use hand claps only. Clap slowly on accented beats. You say each line and the children repeat after you. The clapping continues throughout.

These stories are not meant to be memorized, as the action rhymes are, but they depend on the children listening carefully to your line and then repeating it in the same rhythm. But if the children ever do memorize one of these, it is fun to omit your lines and have, instead, alternate lines of clapping between the children's speaking. In other words, all speak and clap a line together, then clap only, for that same number of beats, then speak and clap the second line, and so forth. It is more fun this way than simply going straight through the story, and it helps improve listening and memory, as the children will be mentally rehearsing the line they just said as they clap the line following it. This gives each individual some practice by himself where he cannot lean on the group.

Memory Verse Rhythms. Memory verses can often be practiced in a rhythm, for easier learning and longer retention. Try stepping the rhythm of Mark 16:15.

GO	ye	IN -	to
ALL	the	WORLD	and
PREACH	the	GOS -	pel to
EV -	ery	CREA -	ture.

Enhance this even more by making newspaper "places." Have each child name a place—Beaver Lake, Central Park, New York, China, and so forth. Print each child's place with a felt pen on a sheet of newspaper. Scatter these about the room. Then everyone says the verse while stepping from place to place about the room. At the end of the verse, comment about the places various children ended on. Repeat several times. Save the newspaper places to use again for reviewing the verse on the following weeks.

These words from Psalm 47:7 have a natural rhythm. Try sitting and standing with them.

```
      GOD    (Stand.)
is the KING  (Sit.)
   of ALL    (Stand.)
the EARTH    (Sit.)
```

Try a choral reading on the rhythm of Exodus 20:11.

```
TEACHER: In SIX DAYS the LORD made
GROUP 1: HEAVEN
GROUP 2: and EARTH,
GROUP 3: the SEA,
ALL GROUPS: and ALL that IN them IS.
```

Memory is enhanced in this last verse, not only by the rhythm, but also by the spatial factor. After you lead your children through this a few times you can ask them to think the verse to themselves. As they are trying to say the verse they will be thinking, for instance, "That side said *heaven,* this side said *and earth,* and the back row said *the sea.*" The positions of the groups will help children remember the order of the words. This memory trick is very ancient, being at least as old as the Greeks. It still works.

Many verses lend themselves to such rhythmic presentations. They don't all need motions or newspaper place games. Some can simply be strongly accented rhythm. In this form a verse is easier to learn than it is without the rhythm. You can easily mold many of your memory verses into a form such as this.

```
JEsus SAID . . .
HE that beLIEVeth on ME
HATH everLASTing LIFE.
```

READING CHECK

1. If singing is omitted in the early years, later learning never quite makes up for it.   T F

2. Most all kindergarten children can carry a tune accurately.   T F

3. If a child makes up his own song he should be led from that to a real song.   T F

4. Children's voices are high and their songs should be pitched rather high.   T F

5. To teach a singing game you should give as few preliminary instructions as possible.   T F

6. There are ways to encourage creativity in the use of rhythm instruments.   T F

7. Rhythm and rhyme act as aids to memory.   T F

7 Movement and Games

- *Why Movement?*
- *Story-Related Movements*
- *Games of Low Organization*
- *Games of Higher Organization*
- *Games for Specific Purposes*

Children of kindergarten age are moving into the game age. Previously, these children can be said to have been in the pre-game stage, where they were not mentally or socially ready for the cooperation required by games. But through the kindergarten years they develop immensely in the abilities required by games.

Why Movement?

Bible teachers like to use games they call "Bible learning" games because of the Bible teaching that can be accomplished in this way. It is true that games can provide repetition and reinforcement of various teachings in a Bible lesson, and this is an important reason for using them. But there are other advantages to the children which may far outweigh these "academic" advantages. Through playing games, children gain self-confidence and self-control, which help them to develop a positive self-concept. Through games, they can develop habits of fair play and good sportsmanship; they can learn to cooperate and get along with others. Through games, children develop mentally. The organization of games, the decision-making, the goals, and other features help children develop their mental powers. Many games require thinking in an active setting; that is, children may "think" with their whole bodies.

Using movement as part of learning, has a long history, reaching back into ancient times. Recent theory along this line takes several forms. Some researchers note the place of perceptual-motor abilities in the early learning of children. As infants explore their world through a *motor* approach (reaching, touching, feeling, etc.), they learn to *perceive,* and their perceptions, in turn, are a basic support of *intellectual* functioning. Getman and Kephart are two researchers and writers taking this approach. The roots of intelligence lying in early motor learning is also a tenet of Piaget's view of intellectual development.

Another view stresses the neurological development that accompanies early motor learning. Notable proponents of this view are Doman and Delacato and their Institutes for the Development of Human Potential based in Philadelphia. According to this view, early movements actually help develop the brain and related neurological functioning necessary to intellectual functioning. Most normal children will automatically go through crawling and other movement stages seen as necessary by this theory. But in cases of neurological damage or deficiency, remedial work can bring about an improvement. This remedial work takes the form of patterned movements and exercises designed to help neurological functioning, and this, in turn, leads to better intellectual functioning.

Another view sees a more direct connection between movement and learning. Teachers holding this view might have their children jump into three circles or hopscotch through three squares to learn the concept three. Or they may trace a sandpaper 3 or glue yarn in a 3-shape to learn the numeral 3.

In Bible learning, the parallel of this would be many of the story movements that teachers practice widely— pretending to build the ark, pretending to be a tree growing, and so forth. Going through the movements is sometimes called motor learning, or kinesthetic learning. It is making use of a sense that in some ways is more powerful than the visual and aural senses so often used in our classrooms. Motor learning uses this kinesthetic sense as a route to the brain or, in short, as a way to learn.

This direct view (of movement —→ learning) is favored by people who are concerned largely with cognitive learning. When they can tie a particular movement to a particular learning they are happy. In the United States James Humphrey and Muska Mosston are proponents of this theory. Bryant J. Cratty has popularized it with his books of active games for learning.

Still one more view should be mentioned, and that is a more indirect view of what movement does for children. It might be called the psychological view, and it comes from researchers in Europe. In these researches, children are seen to gain in their self-concept and other facets of personality by experiencing pleasure and success in physical activities. This personality growth results in increased effort at intellectual tasks. The stronger "self" learns better.

So you can take your choice of theories; they all support the use of physical activity and motor learning. Or you can forget all the theories, and just remember to use activity in your classroom, along with the visual learning which is stressed so much, and the aural learning which is used so much.

Story-Related Movements

It really is quite easy to invent movement activities to go with almost any Bible story. Simply leading the children through the story or a part of it, will promote learning. The children may all be Joseph walking over the hills to look for his brothers. Or they may be the fishermen casting their nets over the side of the boat, and pulling in the fish. Or they may be Ruth, walking behind the reapers and picking up what they leave.

You can lead these activities with an informal line of talk that permits the children to inject ideas of theirs, too. "Let's be Noah and build a boat. First, I think we need to saw a big log into boards . . . . Okay, first we'll cut down a tree. Let's saw and saw and saw until our tree falls down. Now let's use an ax and chop off all the branches. Did you get them all? How about those little ones at the top? . . . Well, that was a lot of work, but our boat is finished. Let's watch all the animals go in. Look up high; I see a giraffe. And what are those little things crawling by? Caterpillars? And lizards? I'm glad you know the name of those; I didn't even know what to call them. It's time for us to go inside. If we sit still and listen, we can hear the rain. Sounds to me like a hard, stormy rain . . . ."

Sometimes be something besides a person. See if you can make your body like a rainbow. Be the boat rocking on the stormy waves. Be the sheep following the shepherd. Be other animals.

The next step from simple story actions is the slightly ritualized story. This is a semi-game—an activity halfway between a game and a story action. Here are two examples of this type.

Running to the Ark. Designate a certain object as the ark. Have the children run to the ark and back to you. Then try other variations that you or the children think of, such as walking, walking backwards, hopping and galloping. (Galloping is running with the same foot always forward.)

A variation of this game is to let each child decide how he will go to the ark. After a child decides, he says, "I am going to take long steps to the ark," "I am going to walk on my toes to the ark," etc. Then he does it.

Joshua and the Soldiers. One child is Joshua. He announces, "We will take the city of Jericho." (Or "Take the city of Ai," or "Help the city of Gibeon.") Help him decide which city, and help him know what to say. Then all the children follow him marching about the room until he leads them back to their seats again. Choose a new Joshua and repeat. Marching music may be played.

The two ritual games just given depend primarily on action. With the addition of more dialogue and chanting, a new dimension—that of language development and speech practice—is added.

Eric came to his kindergarten class and the teacher could hardly understand his speech. Through the year she made much use of rhymes and ritual games such as the following. Eric's special favorite was "Tents for Sale," and he had to pronounce his colors clearly so the tentmakers knew which ones to sell him. By the end of the year Eric went off to first grade speaking almost as well as his classmates.

Room at the Inn. Choose one child to be innkeeper. All the other children may line up at the inn door, which may be a table, side of a piano, or a real door on which they can knock. For a large group have them line up two or more together instead of single file. Explain that one corner or area of the room is the "red room" and another area is the "green room." The first group

145

knocks and says, "Have you any room?" The innkeeper may answer, "No, we haven't any room" in which case the group goes to the end of the line and awaits another turn. Or the innkeeper may answer, "Yes. Which room do you want?" Then he holds out his two closed hands which contain a red and a green button, piece of crayon, or other object. If they choose the hand with the red object they go to the red room. And if they choose the hand with the green object they go to the green room. When everyone is in a room, count the children and see which room has the most. Count slowly and let the children help you.

Tax Money. Distribute "money" in some way to all the children. It could be hidden around the room and the children find as many pieces as they can. It could be handed out as payment while the children are cleaning the room. "Here are two dollars (pounds, coins) for putting away the crayons." "Here are three dollars for carrying that heavy box." Etc. Or it could simply be passed out before this game.

When ready to begin, have the children sit in a circle and count their dollars. Help all those who need it. Then have a Zacchaeus (or Matthew) walk around the inside of the circle saying, "I'm Zacchaeus, the tax collector." He stops in front of a child and asks, "How many dollars do you have to pay your taxes?" The child answers, "I have *(the number in his hand)* dollars to pay my taxes." He pays Zacchaeus. Then he becomes the next tax collector and the game continues.

Tents for Sale. Choose an Aquila and a Priscilla. They will have in their house a number of colored tents (simple tent-shaped pieces cut from construction paper). Other children sit in a circle around the house. All the children, or just Aquila and Priscilla, may chant, "Tents for sale. Tents for sale. Come and buy a tent." Then either Aquila or Priscilla chooses a child to come, saying his name. When the customer comes they ask, "What color tent do you want?" He answers, "I want a *(color)* tent." Aquila and Priscilla give him the color he wants. Or, if they are out of that color, further conversation follows until the customer buys a tent. Then chant again and repeat the whole procedure.

If you wish, this game may be played in a tent made from a sheet or large carton or table or whatever you can manage. Aquila and Priscilla sit in the doorway and the other children come and go more informally, instead of sitting in the circle formation.

Games of Low Organization

Kindergarten children, though they have entered the game stage, will not be adept at cooperative teamwork. They usually are not interested in competition, or in waiting too long for their turns. In short, they are not yet ready for elaborately organized games.

The younger or more immature the children, or the more inexperienced they are at games, the simpler their games should be. Games with low organization for these children are characterized by lack of long term goals, competitive scorekeeping, and too many parts to play. In some games all the children, except perhaps an "It," do the same thing. Some games are teacher-led. "Wins" are achieved at every turn instead of at the end of the game. Here are some examples of games of low organization.

Horse and Chariot. Use jump ropes or bathrobe cords or torn strips of an old sheet or whatever convenient material you can find. Most children will not need to be told how to play Horse and Chariot; it is just like their familiar game of Horse. The chariot rider holds the two ends of the rope and the horse is in front of him with the rope around his chest. The two go galloping and riding wherever they will. Good drivers always are careful, though; they don't bump into things and have accidents.

What is Missing? Have the children sit in a circle. Put a number of objects or pictures in the center of the circle. Tell the children to look carefully at all the things and try to remember what is there. Then have them close their eyes while you take away one of the objects. Have them open their eyes and see if they know what is missing. After they guess return the object and let various children take turns removing one.

May I—Thank You. Tell the children to come to you with requests, as "Teacher, may I touch the door?" or "Teacher, may I play one note on the piano?" or "Teacher, may I sit on the floor?" You answer, "Yes, you may sit on the floor," or "No, you may not hit Tommy." Repeat the whole request in your answer. Each time a child receives a Yes answer he is to say, "Thank you, Teacher." (Or use your name.) Then he may do the thing he has permission to do.

Children find it great fun to be creative in thinking up new things to ask. Play this game informally. Do not take turns or stand in line.

Sentence Game. Cut out several pictures of

people or items from your Bible lesson. Examples: Moses, rod, burning bush, sheep, shoes. Mount the pictures on identical pieces of paper. Turn the pictures face down and scramble them. Let a child select two pictures and try to make a sentence using both words. After his turn he puts his pictures back and mixes all the pictures before the next child takes a turn.

When the children become adept at making a sentence using two words, let them try selecting three pictures.

Fisherman Tag. One child is Fisherman. He tries to tag other children. As each child is tagged he becomes a fisherman and begins helping tag others. When all are fishermen the game is over. The first child tagged becomes the new Fisherman and play resumes.

Other names may be substituted for "fisherman" to relate the game to many Bible stories—for instance, farmer, shepherd, traveler, soldier. A variation of this game is to arrange something which must be removed, instead of tagging a child. It may be ribbon attached to clothing with a bit of tape. When a child loses his ribbon he joins Fisherman in trying to remove ribbons from the others.

Games of Higher Organization

As children mature and become more experienced with games, their games can become more complicated. Circle games and other formations now become possible. But visualizing a circle and cooperating with others to form one may not be easy. Perhaps the simplest way to accomplish this is for you to take hold of the hands of two children and ask the others to join hands and form a circle. As the children imitate you, the circle will

TEACHING KINDERGARTNERS

materialize. For line formations, it is best to actually mark the line with chalk or some other means. Stand on the line yourself and ask the children to do the same. When you choose a child to demonstrate to the others what to do, be sure to choose an alert child who catches on quickly to instructions. If you use a slower child, interest will lag.

When teaching a new game, avoid giving all the instructions at once. Children ordinarily will not be able to hold in their minds the total game before they have experienced it. At the beginning it is best to tell them only enough to get them started, and then add more information as it is needed. The following three steps will be generally useful for teaching games.

1. Organize the children into the game formation—circle, line or whatever is needed.

2. Give a brief explanation of the game. (Many times this step can be omitted and you can move directly to Step 3.)

3. Assist a child or children in the first actions of the game. Or demonstrate by taking the first turn yourself. Continue assisting as needed until the children understand well enough to proceed by themselves.

Following are some games with higher organization than those in the previous section. Compare Fisherman Tag to Shepherd Tag to see some of the differences. You will notice in the latter game that the children have a specific place to run as they avoid getting tagged, whereas in the former game they have only the one job of trying not to be tagged. Compare Concentration with What Is Missing? In the simpler game the children try for one turn to remember a picture. In the higher-level game they continue trying to remember from turn to turn, and they have the additional job of trying to find a match for each picture. Compare Concentration also to the Sentence Game. In the Sentence Game a child can turn over any two pictures successfully; there is no way to fail in this. Then he makes a sentence, which he can practically always do, or if not you can help him. But in concentration he should think and make decisions before turning over the cards. Even if he doesn't think and just plays by chance, he has to think afterward and make a decision about whether he gets to keep the cards.

When you are aware of the kinds of factors that make a game easier or more difficult for children you will find it easy to make adjustments in games as needed for your group. Game rules are not passed down from on high and you can do whatever you want with them once you get them into your classroom.

Here are several games which have somewhat higher organization than those in the previous section.

Shepherd Tag. Select a goal line. Choose one child to be a shepherd. He says, "I'm going to hunt bears" (or wolves, or lions). The other children are the bears. They fall in line behind the shepherd, and he marches around in any direction, with the others following him. When the shepherd has them all away from the goal line he calls, "I see bears!" The bears run to the goal and the shepherd catches as many as he can. The shepherd chooses a new shepherd from the children who were not caught.

Concentration. Prepare two matching sets of picture cards from your Bible lesson. Example: Peter, boat, net, fish, Jesus. Mount the pictures on identical pieces of paper. Turn the pictures face down and scramble them. Let a child select two pictures. If they match he keeps them and takes another turn. If they do not match he turns them down again and another child takes a turn.

Poor Donkey. Have the children stand in a circle holding hands. Choose one child to be Balaam. Let him stand inside the circle to start the game. Another child, the donkey, stands outside. Balaam tries to catch the donkey by going under the children's clasped hands. The donkey can go in and out of the circle in the same manner. The children try to protect the donkey by raising and lowering their clasped hands. When Balaam finally catches the donkey everyone says, "Poor donkey," and the game starts again with two more players.

Games for Specific Purposes

Any particular game actually accomplishes many more purposes than the one for which it may have been chosen and included in a lesson plan. For instance, a teacher may choose "Joshua and the Soldiers" simply to reinforce in an active way a fact from the lesson. But the concomitant learnings are likely to be more numerous and possibly more important than the planned learning. The children will learn to observe the leader, to follow, to cooperate with others in a common endeavor. As leader, a child may exhibit creativity in trying to think of a new route or new place to go. Coordination in marching may be improved, and the feel for a marching rhythm.

Since games have such multiple results it is difficult to try to classify them. The classification in the previous two sections has to do with the difficulty level. But games might also be classified according to whether they are largely for physical development or verbal development or for thinking. They might also be classified as indoor or outdoor, team or individual, large group or small group, competitive or cooperative, and many other arrangements.

Here, we will discuss just two additional types. One type of game, which is rather a newcomer on the scene is the cooperative game. People who object to a competitive society, promote cooperative games as an alternative way to raise children.

An example of a cooperative game is this adaptation of Musical Chairs. Each time the music stops and all the children race for chairs, they are supposed to help each other. Instead of one or more children being left out and thus disappointed, all are supposed to share the remaining chairs. Two might sit side by side on a chair, or three or four pile on each other's laps. There is a lot of giggling and fun with this. It probably is more fun to squeeze five onto a chair than to sit alone and successful in the old style of the game. And no one is disappointed in being left out. The success of this game demonstrates that kindergarten children are not really ready for highly competitive games.

Games which really are learning drills or review drills are popular in our cognitively-oriented society. Here are four examples of this type.

Action Review. Make two preparations for this game. (1) Prepare a list of questions which have a choice of only two answers. The choices may be Yes and No, or they may be choices between two persons such as David and Jonathan, or Mary and Martha. (2) Devise two kinds of actions and specify that one action indicates a particular answer and the other action indicates the opposite answer. Some possibilities are: raise right hand or raise left hand, stand or sit, run to this corner or run to that corner, jump into this circle or jump into that circle.

Ask questions and, if possible, have all the children answer at once. If your group is too large for all to do the more active answers you may let several children at a time show the answers. The other children will be "observers" who raise their hands if an answer is correct.

Drawing Review. Prepare several questions which can be answered with a simple drawing. Ask the questions one at a time and let the children draw their answers. Some examples are:

1. What did Mary put baby Jesus in? (manger)
2. What did the shepherds take care of ? (sheep)
3. What did the shepherds see one night? (angels)
4. What did the shepherds find in a manger? (Baby Jesus)

The children may all draw at their seats on paper or Magic Slates or individual chalkboards, and then hold up their drawings for you to see. Or you may call on volunteers to come to a chalkboard in front of the group and draw the answer while the other children watch.

Stick Man Review. Have ready a list of questions you want your children to be able to answer. When they answer one question draw the head of a stick man, when they answer a second question draw his body. Continue until all eight parts are drawn.

The man may be said to represent a Bible character the children are learning about, such as Moses, or Peter.

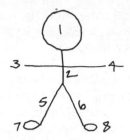

Listen and Clap. Slowly say a list of words. Have the children listen for one which goes with the day's Bible lesson. When they hear one they should respond by clapping, jumping up, or any other predetermined action. Make your own list of words similar to this example: Tom, Bill, *David;* ball, jump rope, bicycle, *sling;* etc. Rhyme adds another dimension to this game. Example: stranger, *manger;* car, jar, *star,* etc.

READING CHECK

1. Learning by movement is definitely secondary to learning by seeing.   T   F

2. The best use of games is as an interlude between real learning activities.   T   F

3. It is all right to change game rules for your class. T   F

4. Games of lower organization have shorter term goals and fewer parts to play than more highly organized games.
                                                                        T   F

5. Kindergarten children are not yet mentally or socially ready for highly competitive games.   T   F

6. Research shows that games promote learning primarily in the physical realm.   T   F

Answers: 1—F, 2—F, 3—T, 4—T, 5—T, 6—F

8 Classroom and Lesson Materials

- *How Shall We Use Learning Centers?*
- *Areas and Centers*
- *Other Aspects of Room Environment*
- *Evaluating Curriculum Materials*
- *Using Published Lessons*

In our churches today kindergarten classrooms are coming more and more to resemble those of the public schools and other day schools. In some respects this is good, but in other respects it may not be. We may have been too quick to adopt certain secular school practices because they are "educational," whereas if we had taken more time to examine the new practices in the light of our Christian education purposes we might not have been so convinced of their value for us. Or if we had taken more time to integrate the new practices into our purposes, we could make better use of them. In a day when the majority of children attend weekday kindergartens, and a good many attend preschools too, there really is no point in our duplicating these programs on Sunday.

How Shall We Use Learning Centers?

One of the major movements in recent years is toward more use of learning centers. This practice has been adopted so unthinkingly in some churches that children spend a good portion of the Sunday school hour building with blocks, playing house, working puzzles and so forth, just as in their weekday schools. True, the teachers may be trying to get the children to "build the walls like Nehemiah," or to say table grace before they pretend to eat in the toy kitchen. But these efforts are largely unsuccessful, being tacked on to the real play of the children, being imposed by the teacher instead of played out by the children.

It is a rare teacher who makes use of centers and play areas as the teacher in the opening chapter of this book. In her well-taught and well-planned unit on Bible families, the centers were making a genuine contribution, and if they were not she would remove them, as she explained with the blocks.

The widespread use of centers has made for happy, busy classrooms, and certainly there can be no claim that this has harmed the children. And if the centers were removed some teachers would be at a loss to fill the time profitably.

But while the learning center movement has been growing with much fanfare, another movement has also quietly been growing. That is the movement toward a longer, teacher-led, group learning time. Teachers are learning that they need not be limited to one story per session. They are learning a wider variety of games, rhymes, movement activities, and other ways to teach children in groups. They are learning more ways to practice memory verses, and they are becoming more skilled in directing group conversational times. A teacher skilled at leading kindergarten groups is reluctant to give up too much of the brief Sunday school hour to learning center activities.

The choices you need to make in your own church are complicated. You must consider the children you minister to. Do they attend preschools and kindergartens during the week? Do they have blocks and puzzles and toy stoves to play with in their homes? Are they mostly from Christian homes, or is your hour with them the only Bible teaching they are receiving? You also need to consider the available space, facilities and money in your church. It takes more space and more expense to provide elaborate learning areas and centers, but ingenious teachers can provide some learning centers in almost any space.

Perhaps most of all you need to consider your own convictions about the best way to teach. Your mind, of course, should always be open to new ideas. You should not be afraid to experiment, and you should from time to time stretch out into new areas. But for the present time you will do best what you thoroughly believe in now. Lay hold of new ideas slowly. Integrate them into your total thinking.

Many Sunday school departments have been ruined by someone who went off to a seminar or workshop and came back and said, "Hey, we're doing it all wrong." If that someone happens to be in charge, he often proceeds to upset everything as he institutes his newly-learned ideas. New, young Christian education directors, fresh out of school, sometimes do the same thing. When the dust settles from such an upheaval the department has lost all or most of the faithful teachers who have loved the children for so long, and in older youth departments may also have lost up to ninety percent of the students as well. Kindergarten children are not as able to object by their absence as the youth are, but we can surely know they are affected.

Some years ago when open schools were the newest fad in education the buildings were built, and the faculties assembled to plan the freedom for the children. Then the doors were opened and the children walked into their great, new freedom, but a good many of them didn't know how to handle it. Some strange stories have come out of that era. There's the girl, for instance, who spent the first three months in the restroom. It probably was the only place where things went on in their old familiar way.

It works much more successfully to teach children a step at a time how to use their freedom. In the case of learning centers, introduce them one at a time, and help children learn to use the equipment and materials by themselves. Then you can gradually widen the choices available to them without bringing chaos.

Areas and Centers

To be really technical about it, there is a difference between areas and centers. Areas are more permanent, although they can be rearranged. The two major areas used in Sunday schools are the rug or circle area where the children and teacher meet for most large group activities, and the worktable area where the children do their handwork. In larger Sunday schools there may also be a library area, a play area (with toy furniture, dress-up clothes and so forth), a paint area, a nature area, and a block area.

Some of the areas, such as the nature area, can be reduced to centers, so there is not a hard and fast line between what should be an area and what should be a center. But thinking in terms of the major areas of your room can help you plan how to use it most efficiently. Are the worktables near the chalkboard, for instance, so you can demonstrate things? Are they near the pin-up space where children will display their work? And how accessible are they to the supplies the children need to get and put away?

If you have a piano in your room is it near the circle area? What view do the children have as they sit in their circle or group? Do they face the door so they see the secretary come for the offering basket, or do they face bright sunlight with you silhouetted against it?

Is the library area in a quiet corner, or is it next to the noisy blocks? Do either the readers or the block builders have to operate in an area where traffic constantly crosses?

Any housewife who enjoys arranging her home can do well in arranging the classroom areas when she puts a little thought to it. And when problems become evident, she can always rearrange. In larger rooms with larger classes it is good to use various kinds of barriers and dividers. Research shows that the noise level of the children tends to be lower in such a room than in a completely open room.

Interest centers or learning centers are more flexible. They take less space and can be arranged within the areas. A nature center, for instance, can be as small as a shelf or windowsill in the library area. Various kinds of art centers can be set up on the worktables or on any floor space. A center may even take the form of a set of pictures on a wall.

Centers often are planned to go with a particular unit of learning and then are changed to go with a new unit. But centers also can be used to create interest in some unrelated topic. The current unit may be on the Bible or the church, but if the autumn leaves are at the height of their glory the teacher may want to bring some in and help her children enjoy God's beautiful handiwork and praise Him for it, even if she can't fit it into the unit. Many other things will also be worth learning and enjoying for their own sake; life is far broader than classroom units and lesson aims.

Here are some other centers that can be used. Listing them here is not necessarily a recommendation that each of these should be used in a Sunday school or church program. Instead, the list is intended to indicate some of the wide variety of things which interest kindergartners. You should choose only what fits your own teaching purposes.

Coloring center. Sometimes have crayons, sometimes felt-tip pens, and occasionally colored chalk, and of course paper to draw on and color on.

161

Cut and paste center. Colored paper and other "beautiful junk." Scissors, paper, paste, paste brushes, and wet paper towels for clean-up complete this center.

Dress-up center. Store clothes in a chest or hang them on hooks and hangers. Have clothes for Bible time people and for modern day people. Police hats, firemen's hats, nurses' hats are popular. A full-length mirror is important. In some neighborhoods such a center is the only place where children see themselves at full length.

Finger painting center. Should be near a sink. Use homemade or commercial finger paint. Paint on wet butcher paper. Or paint on a cookie sheet and when you like the design transfer it to paper by pressing it all over and then gently lifting it.

Listening center. Tape or record player, tapes, and headphones. Teacher-made tapes are often better than commercial ones because you can tailor-make them for your children. You can read stories, sing new songs your class is learning, and give instructions for doing worksheets.

Music center. This can also have listening equipment with earphones. Have tone bells, xylophones, or jars to tune with water. Rhythm instruments can sometimes be available. Let the children have experience producing and listening to a variety of tones and sounds.

Needlework center. The ancient Israelites did beautiful needlework for the tabernacle. Your children can embroider designs and pictures on burlap with yarn and large needles. Simple looms can teach them about weaving. Scraps can be sewn together for all kinds of uses. These materials can also be stored on shelves, or in a box.

Painting center. An easel constitutes a center, but children also can paint on tables or floor. Clean-up facilities should be nearby and the children taught to do their own cleaning. They also should wear paint smocks.

Sometimes try spatter painting or print making for a change from brush painting.

Picture center. Old Sunday school papers, Christmas cards and magazines should be available for cutting out pictures. These might be used for ambitious projects such as bulletin boards or scrapbooks, or they may simply be cut out for the pleasure of cutting out a nice picture.

Puppet center. A large carton or a table turned on its side can make a theatre. Puppets can be commercial, or children can make their own. Teach appropriate behavior for both audience and performers.

Sand play center. A sand table or floor box can be partially filled with cornmeal or beans or grain of some kind, or even with sand, although sand is harder on floors and carpets. A rug underneath helps protect floors and makes cleanup easier. Bible stories can at times be acted out with toy people, camels, houses and so forth. Some teachers have decided that sand is too messy for indoors, and they set theirs up outside.

Storyboard center. Flannelgraph figures and felt cutouts can be used for telling stories, making pictures, spelling names, and other profitable activities.

Table game and manipulative center. Matching games, sorting games, puzzles and similar items are used here for individual learning. Cheerios and other items for stringing and sorting are also useful. All these items should probably be stored on shelves and brought to a table at the time of use. Clay might be here or in a separate center, with cookie cutters, popsicle sticks and other items to use with the clay, and with newspaper or plastic for protecting the table.

Viewing center. Use filmstrip projector, Viewmaster, or any kind of viewing equipment. Turn a table on its side for a theatre. Rules for using listening and viewing equipment need to be firmly enforced.

Water play center. A baby bathtub or other container

should be filled only about one-third full of water. Boats and fishing nets make good Sea-of-Galilee play. Baby dolls and washcloths fit Bible baby stories. Spoons, plastic bottles with and without holes, funnels, sponges and other water paraphernalia add immeasurably to the fun.

Here are some space-saving ideas for setting up centers in small rooms.

Put up clothesline to hang wet projects or to hold finished pieces for children.

Install narrow-lipped
shelves on a wall in
your room or hallway.

If you build a work top
against a wall it takes less
space than an ordinary
table.

Make access to paper
easier by fixing a
large roll to the
wall.

You can hinge work tops to the wall. These double as bulletin boards, and save space.

If you build a work top against a wall it takes less space than an ordinary table.

Hinge cupboard doors to the wall and have two surfaces for displaying books or pictures.

Sometimes let the children stand while working. It takes up less space than chairs.

Using sides of cardboard boxes makes it easy to build easels for young children.

If you look around your room, you may find spare storage space.

By using centers you can plan something to challenge every child in your room. The wide range of abilities and interests can all be met.

One teacher was in a small cell of a room where she did not even have space for a circle area and a table area. The children sat around the table to listen to the story and then did their handwork at the same table. And she had Bret, who was a behavior problem. He needed training in manners, but he also needed special intellectual challenge, as he was brighter than most in the class and had been learning to read. The teacher decided to capitalize on his interest in reading and she read some Bible stories onto tape, saying, "Turn to the next page," at the proper times so Bret could more easily follow along in the book as he listened. Bret was delighted with his private listening center. He listened when he arrived early, he listened when he finished his handwork ahead of the others, and he even listened many times instead of doing his handwork, since he found the reading more challenging. Bret learned to give other children turns (his manners were improving) and he tried to teach them how to follow in the book, but they all lost interest quickly, and in the end Bret had the tapes all to himself.

Finding something that truly interests and stimulates the Brets in your class will tax your ingenuity at times, but it is far better than struggling to make them conform in activities that are not right for them. A rich learning environment with a variety of learning centers can help you do this.

Learning centers should be changed often. When children lose interest in one set of materials, put them away for a while and put out something new. When one unit of work is finished clear away the materials associated with it, and change the classroom scenery. A stale interest center is like a Christmas tree still standing in February.

Other Aspects of Room Environment

Some of the advice we are given about kindergarten rooms is conflicting. On one hand we are told we should have beautiful rooms to attract children by their aesthetic appeal, and on the other hand we are told to have learning centers, supplies available on open shelves, children's work displayed, and space for storing half-finished work. The clutter of this latter type of room is enough to make a neatnik teacher decide kindergarten teaching is not for her. On one hand we are told that children need the stimulation of a rich learning environment, but on the other hand there are children so distracted by such clutter that they are severely handicapped in their learning.

What is a teacher to do? Most of them want beautiful rooms and fight clutter but grow more and more immune to it. They become collectors and hoarders as they see ways to use practically anything in their kindergarten rooms. The room comes to look quite different to the teacher and children who live in it than it does to the casual visitor. The sloppily painted sheet hanging on the line, the shelf full of poorly-fitted paper houses, the boxes of scraps, the brushes standing in cups of half-dried paint, the unsorted crayons, the paintings and drawings and pastings all over the walls, some nice and straight, obviously hung by the teacher, and some obviously taped up by the children—all these are the stuff of life to those who live in the room. Heart and soul have gone into the work. Dreams hang on it. Some can hardly wait until the sheethouse is dry and they can crawl inside. Accomplishments, growing, disappointments, friends. The clutter of life.

Sometimes a neatnik manages to leave a sparkling room behind, but the others have never yet figured out how it is done.

In secular education, space recommendations range from 35 square feet per child on up to about 60. In a more

169

limited, Sunday-only program probably not quite as much space is needed. But one thing is sure, the overwhelming majority of church kindergarten rooms need more space than they have.

Bulletin boards and chalkboards should be child height. Pictures should be hung child height. Shelves— there never seem to be enough of those. Open shelves and closed shelves. Many shelves so children can store things easily; they can't manage it if too much crowding is required. High shelves for the teacher. Keep everything not immediately needed by the children in your own storage area and put out for them only current materials.

Chairs can range from 10 to 13 inches in seat height, with most of them being 11 and 12 inches high. A full saddle seat and a lumbar support about 8 inches above the seat are best. The chair should be sturdy and broad based, but should not weigh more than 8 or 10 pounds. Children need to be able to carry the chairs easily and safely. Chairs designed so they stack will save space.

Table surfaces should be about 7 to 8 inches higher than the chair seats. Tables covered with linoleum or formica or other plastic coatings resist wear better than varnished or painted surfaces. Table corners should be rounded to help avoid injury from the corners.

Furniture in the library area should have a different look from the rest of the room. Rockers, beanbag chairs, pillows can be used. An old springs and mattress can be covered to resemble a couch. A washing machine carton to crawl into provides a delightfully private place to look at books.

The room really needs a sink, and a drinking fountain would be great. Restrooms immediately adjacent to the kindergarten room are much better than having some down the hall. This allows for easier and better supervision of children at all times. Few church kindergartens are now equipped this way, but more and more are learning what is needed, and we see much better kindergarten facilities these days than we did only a few years ago.

It is ideal if the kindergarten room is on the ground floor and if it has its own exit to the outdoor play area. This, again, allows for better supervision and more flexible scheduling. It eliminates the necessity of having to herd children through halls for their time of outdoor activity.

Outdoor play equipment is seeing a quiet revolution. On the old style slide a child climbed alone up the steep stairs, and he wasn't allowed to dawdle because of the line of impatient children behind him. He reached the tiny platform and stood there—alone—because there was room for only him. Then he sat down and slid in the only way allowed. The slide was steep, so the rules permitted no head-first, or backward sliding or anything else creative. A timid or poorly coordinated child might get hurt with some of these exciting variations, so even the brave children—who never get hurt—are not allowed to try them.

The new style slide is likely to be low and wide. A large platform allows congregating of friends. Three of them might decide to slide down together.

Other one-use pieces of equipment are giving way to multi-use equipment. Some of the very best playgrounds are those built by groups of parents who use their imaginations and the material available to them. A truck driver may bring a couple of giant truck tires. They are for walking around the top, bouncing on, or sitting in. They can become forts or houses or stores. A welder or plumber may put together a uniquely-shaped jungle gym. A carpenter may add a playhouse. Logs or beams to sit on or walk along, culverts to crawl through, sawhorses, planks, shovels, rakes—all these are popular with kindergarten children. Wheeled toys, ropes, balls, a tree to climb. No longer is the ground leveled off flat. A hill may be the most popular piece of play equipment. One section of the playground may be sand. Another may be available for planting a garden. Variety is the word. Anything goes—that is, anything the parents can think up and the children enjoy that seems safe enough to the powers that be.

Evaluating Curriculum Materials

The main thing to know about evaluations is that they are only as good as the evaluator. There are a number of do-it-yourself systems being circulated, and these usually consist of some kind of check list. A check list in the hands of a qualified person can give some good information.

When you consider buying a second-hand car, one option open to you in many cities is to take it to an auto analyst. The analyst performs tests and examinations and jots information on his prepared list. Then he sits down with you and goes over each item on the list, explaining what he found, making interpretations about what it might mean in the way of repairs or cost of operation or other considerations, and answering your questions about things you don't understand.

Since the analyst is a highly qualified specialist in autos, you can have confidence in the information you receive from him. But you are not likely to consider passing out forms to your artist and banker friends, or even to amateur mechanics that you know. If you did, the information you received from them would be only as good as their knowledge of cars. Some questions almost anyone could answer by looking at the car, some questions the "lay" mechanic will happen to know the answer to, and some questions only the specialist could answer for you.

That is exactly the situation with the ordinary check list on curriculum. A common question on these lists is, "Do the materials fit the age levels of the children?" One

Christian education professor was asked how he handled that question. How did he teach his students to go about answering it? He said, "I don't. I have to leave that to the curriculum specialists. I can't know enough about every age, and my students can't either, especially at this point in their lives."

Now of course there are some lessons still appearing that are poorly geared to the various age levels and have other kinds of problems, but most publishers today are producing excellent lessons. Never in the history of Christian education has there been such a selection of high quality materials. There is a wide range of what is "good" educationally, and check lists that have you look for this or that detail of lesson format are not only useless, they at times can be misleading by failing to draw your attention to more important, underlying principles in the curriculum you are examining.

Unless you have the equivalent of an auto analyst in education in your church, you are better off to do as the professor advises his students, and leave the educational aspects to the publishers. Rely on their track record, other satisfied users, qualifications of their curriculum personnel and so forth.

But in the area of Bible and theology every church has at least one qualified analyst—the pastor. There may be others too. It is important that the lessons you choose come from a publisher whose doctrinal stand is the same as your church's. If your denomination has its own publishing house this may be the choice for you. But, unfortunately, some of these smaller publishing houses are the ones who lack high educational quality and a larger one may have lost theological touch with some segments of its sprawling denomination. So this is not the answer for every church. Non-denominational publishers may not be able to emphasize in their lessons certain teachings which your church considers important. So there are many complicated theological matters to consider, and the best analyst in your church should take the job of evaluating which curriculum best fits your church from a doctrinal standpoint.

A weakness in the educational program of a good many Sunday schools today is what might be called curriculum hopping. In three or four years a Sunday school might switch curriculums three or four times and often for rather frivolous reasons. One teacher may be dissatisfied because it isn't like what she was used to in her former church and she raises a fuss. Or someone has just learned in college by a check list that such and such curriculum is the "best." Often these are the very people who change their minds when someone shows them a new feature of another curriculum. A common reason for a switch is that someone heard a rumor that such and such a publishing house is going "liberal."

Producing a curriculum is a massive job and it is not possible for your curriculum materials to change drastically overnight, and it is not possible for quality to shift so much that you need to change every year or so in order to keep on top. Sunday schools would be better off not to switch curriculums at the drop of each new fad. Once a curriculum is chosen for good, solid reasons, then bend your efforts toward using it as it is meant to be used. Realize that problems in the Sunday schools have many causes, and switching curriculums again is not usually the solution.

Using Published Lessons

The first thing to do when you receive new lessons from your publisher, is to study the teacher's manual thoroughly. Study it until you know what the lessons are designed to accomplish, how they will accomplish it, how the class period is arranged, and how the classroom is to be organized.

The second thing to do is try it. This suggestion is important because many teachers have been frustrated and discouraged because lessons from a new publisher their Sunday school has switched to do not work with the scheduling and methods they are used to from a former publisher or from some training class they attended. As an example, some teachers are used to talking to their children for twenty or thirty minutes—telling the Bible story and interspersing it with sermonizing, moralizing, and other teaching they want to accomplish. Then they are given lessons that present the Bible story more briefly and follow it up with learning activities which require participation by the children. These teachers often are frustrated to find they are not given as much "sermon" material and, being inexperienced in using activities for learning, they skip those. Thus they end up with an unsatisfactory lesson.

Published lessons are a major source of teacher training at the present time. They tell what to do, they give much help in how to do it, and sometimes they even explain why it is good to do it that way. A teacher who studies the material and tries to work it can learn a lot. When there are new methods and new ideas, they may need to be tried more than once. Both children and teacher need time to adjust to new ways.

Too often a teacher tries something once, says "My children can't do that," and then falls back again to something familiar and comfortable—perhaps the same three or four songs the children know and have been singing for a couple of years. But the whole job of teaching is to continually lead children into new experiences and new learnings. If your children can't do it, there is challenge for you to help them learn it. If they can do it, then there's nothing for you to teach. This is not to say you should tackle things which are beyond the abilities of kindergarten children to learn, but you should tackle things which they simply haven't learned.

Other teachers, receiving the new lessons as in the situation described earlier, study them thoroughly, try out the new kinds of activities and are delighted with the results. They see their discipline problems falling away, their children learning more, and their own teaching horizons being stimulated and enriched.

Inexperienced teachers can lean heavily on such published materials, which not only provide the curriculum for them, but also provide much in the way of teacher training. Experienced teachers lean on them for the timesaving features. It is the experienced teachers who know best how much thought, work, time, and expertise go into planning a good lesson, and they are glad in their busy lives for the help of prepared lessons.

But published lessons are not to be followed slavishly. After you know the lessons and understand the purposes, and have well in mind your own aims, then you are ready to make adjustments. For lack of time, something may need to be cut. Because of space or equipment limitations something may need to be changed. For a handicapped child some adjustments will be needed.

As each child is unique, so each class develops its own personality. An activity that this year's class loves to do may not catch on at all with next year's class. And you have the ever-challenging job of teaching each class as it is. Whatever the needs and problems, they are yours to work with. The good lessons published today are your best tool, but they cannot do the job without you.

READING CHECK

1. Room areas are more permanent, while learning centers should be changed more often.   T F

2. A wide variety of learning centers are appropriate for kindergarten children.   T F

3. Learning centers are necessary for a good Sunday school program.   T F

4. Probably the most important consideration in choosing curriculum is its doctrinal position.   T F

5. Educational excellence in materials is hard to find these days.   T F

6. Best results are obtained by following the lesson suggestions as much as possible, and adapting as necessary for your situation.   T F

Appendix

In this section are study helps for each chapter, which can be used when this book is studied in classrooms or in church training groups.

CHAPTER 1: MEET THE KINDERGARTNER

Questions *(for discussion or for essay topics)*
1. Do you think Sunday schools you have seen need to offer a more activity-oriented program in kindergarten? Why or why not?
2. Do you think teachers need different aims for different children? Give examples to support your answer.
3. Do you think teachers should encourage or discourage sex role differences? Why?

Study Projects
1. Read more about the young child's thought in a book by Piaget or about Piaget theory. Report to your study group what you learn.
2. Find something about the young child's thinking written by Bruner or Almy or another researcher. Report to your study group what you learn.

Observations
1. Observe two or more children involved in the same activity. Jot down differences you notice in the way they work.

2. Observe a kindergarten class. Watch not only the formal teaching, but any small, incidental happenings. Try to find an incident that can affect a child's mental growth, and one which can affect a child's social-emotional growth. Describe each.

Mini-Teaching Experiences

1. Try the doll experiment or one of the bead experiments with one or more kindergarten children.

2. With one child of kindergarten age read a book or play a game or any activity he will like. Share your experience with others in your group, telling what you learned about the sentences and grammar the child uses, his enjoyment of words, his activity level, and any other characteristics you notice.

CHAPTER 2: BIBLE LEARNING

Questions

1. When you were a child, did someone ever use a symbol to teach you an abstraction? What do you remember about that experience?

2. What do you believe about the standing of little children before God? How do you support this belief from the Bible?

3. What terminology do you prefer to use in talking with young children about salvation? Why?

4. Use the story of Joseph or any other story your group chooses and make lists of ideas you think appropriate and inappropriate for kindergarten children to learn. Try to agree on one or two major ideas you would emphasize if you were to use this story in teaching.

Study Projects

1. Talk with one or more kindergarten children

about one of the Bible topics discussed in this chapter. Try to understand what the child is really thinking. Look behind the words he uses, and avoid attaching your adult meanings to his words. Write what you think is the child's definition of the item or person talked about.

2. Interview one or more people who were saved at kindergarten age, and see what they remember about their knowledge at the time. (Such memories, though helpful, are not conclusive about children's thinking since people tend to adjust early memories as their minds mature and later learning changes their thinking.)

Classroom Observations

1. Work with a partner on mini-teaching experience number 1 below. As one partner leads the discussion, the other can be listing the bad and good things the children mention. Or use a tape recorder and make the lists later from a tape. What can you learn from these lists?

2. Observe a kindergarten class as they listen to a Bible story and then discuss it with their teacher. Jot down things you notice about the children's part in the discussion.

Mini-Teaching Experience

Spend a few minutes with a kindergarten class conversing about what is bad to do and what is good to do. Aim to develop some specific plans before the conversation comes to a close. The children can plan happy surprises for someone in their families. If you cannot arrange to use a class, try the same thing with one or two children.

CHAPTER 3: ABOUT STORIES

Questions

1. Can you think of a story that was particularly

meaningful to you as a child? What can you remember about its impact on you?

2. Do you think we should use only those Bible stories that we know will meet some particular need of a child? Why or why not?

3. Do you think we can usually know the effect stories have on children? Should we? Give reasons for your answers.

Study Projects

1. Read something from Bettelheim's book, *The Uses of Enchantment* (Knopf). Report to your study group something important that you learn from it.

2. Analyze a story from a kindergarten Sunday school book or take-home paper—either a Bible story or other kind. Does it seem written to help the child live the story and identify with one of its characters, or does it try too hard to "teach" or moralize? What other comments can you make about the story and its adaptation to kindergarten level?

Observations

1. Observe a class as they listen to a Bible story. Choose one child to watch in particular and make notes on his behavior. Does he wiggle, talk, listen constantly, listen at times? What seems to catch his attention best? Can he answer questions afterward?

2. Observe a kindergarten child as you or someone else reads a story or picture book to him and talks with him about it. What seems to appeal to him the most? Did he learn new words or new ideas? Did he misunderstand? Were there any big words? How did the child react to them?

Mini-Teaching Experiences

1. Find or write a participation story and use it with a group of kindergarten children. What do you notice

about the children's attention?

2. Present a story in any form you choose—puppet, picture book, chalk or other. Afterward have the children retell it or talk about it so you can try to determine their understanding of it.

CHAPTER 4: MORE ABOUT STORIES

Questions

1. Do you think we can usually know the effect stories have on children? Should we always try to? Give reasons for your answers. Has your opinion changed at all as you studied chapters 3 and 4 of this book, and experienced stories with children?

2. Do you remember your school teachers reading stories to your class? Did you enjoy them? How late in elementary school did this continue?

3. Which do you prefer to do—read or tell stories? Why?

Study Projects

1. Read a book on storytelling by Ruth Sawyer or another good storyteller. Comment about whether or not you think all Sunday school teachers ought to prepare a story in this way for each lesson. Discuss with your study group other items that you learned from the book.

2. Collect a small pile of picture books and analyze them. Are they story, mood or participation books? Are the pictures clear enough to use with a group? Do they seem right for kindergarten ages? What else can you learn from examining the books?

3. If you can find two teachers with opposing views on reading stories versus telling stories in a kindergarten Bible class, interview each and find the reasons they give for their beliefs.

Observations

1. Visit a library children's story hour. (Remember, you may be seeing either a professional or an amateur volunteer.) Do you see anything that you think could be used in Sunday school classrooms?

2. Visit a story time in a weekday kindergarten in either a public or private school. What do you learn from this?

Mini-Teaching Experience

Choose and prepare one or more stories, and read them to a group of kindergarten children. With at least one of the stories, help the children talk about it. What can you say about the children's attention and their learning?

CHAPTER 5: TEACHING WITH ART

Questions

1. What do you think about children taking home their art or handwork? Is this important? What purpose(s) does it serve? If children forget and leave their artwork behind, does this mean the work time spent on it was not worthwhile? Is the process of working on it more important, or is the finished product more important?

2. Do you feel you are creative or uncreative in the art-related tasks in your life? (Remember this includes such things as planning your yard, choosing curtains, and arranging your office, as well as painting pictures.) Can you remember childhood experiences that either stifled or encouraged your creativity? What were they?

3. What do you think are the most important values of handwork in a kindergarten Sunday school class?

4. In relation to the value(s) you expressed for question 3, what type of handwork or art activities should be included in the class?

Study Projects

1. Interview one or more kindergarten Sunday school teachers about why they use art in their classes. If possible also interview a public school kindergarten teacher about art. Share the views you hear with your study group.

2. Gather several children's drawings of people, and try to arrange them in order from the simplest to most advanced. You may wish to include pictures from preschool and primary children in this study in order to get a wider range.

3. Gather drawings from a class of kindergarten children. Sort the ones you can according to 1) symbols only, 2) possibly relating symbols to each other, and 3) pictures in which several symbols are obviously related.

4. Analyze one or more published kindergarten handwork sheets. Tell what values you see in each, what weakness you see, and how you might improve it.

Observations

1. Watch some children as they draw on blank paper and listen to their comments as they work. Try to find a child in the manipulative stage, and a child in the representative stage.

2. Watch a group of children engaged in any kind of art work and write out one or two incidents you observe in which some kind of growth seems to be happening in a child—in aesthetic awareness, observation powers, increased skill, or confidence, or other area.

Mini-Teaching Experiences

1. Conduct an art experience related to a real object or to pictures. For instance, bring some flowers. Let each child handle one, smell it, talk about how God made its beautiful colors, shape, size and so forth. Or bring a bird nest and pictures of birds. Talk about them. Then let the

children draw or make flowers, birds or nests.

2. Conduct a handwork time using a published lesson sheet. Try to allow for individuality and creative use of the sheet. Try to make it as meaningful to the children as you can.

CHAPTER 6: MUSIC AND RHYMES

Questions

1. Why do you think some teachers lack confidence in teaching music? What can you suggest to help overcome this?

2. What songs or rhymes do you remember from your childhood? How do you account for remembering these so long?

3. In what ways can singing games contribute to Bible lessons? Do you think they are potentially as valuable as handwork for some lessons? Why or why not?

Study Projects

1. Find some rhymes in a rhyme book or in kindergarten lesson books. Analyze them according to difficulty. Which ones can kindergarten children learn easily and which ones will be difficult? Why? If possible, try these out on some kindergarten children and see if you were correct in your analysis.

2. Discover an old song which you think is appropriate for kindergartners. Look through the hymn book or other sources of songs used by adults in your church and try to find a song or chorus that would be meaningful and singable for kindergartners. Adapt it slightly, if necessary.

3. Choose one or two lesson topics and make up a singing game to go with each one. Use a familiar tune such as "Mary Had a Little Lamb," or make up your own

tune if you wish.

Classroom Observation

Observe a kindergarten music time. Choose one child to watch and report on. Comment on any details you notice—for instance, how much he participates, how well he carries a tune, when his attention wanders, what catches his attention again, what does he seem to like best, and so forth.

Mini-Teaching Experience

Prepare and present a seven-minute session of songs and rhymes. To make a good session, have some which are familiar to the children and try at least one new song and one new rhyme. Have variety—some movement, a bit of conversation about a song, something with the children's names in it, and so forth.

CHAPTER 7: MOVEMENT AND GAMES

Questions

1. Do you see games as belonging primarily to the teaching or to the recreational aspect of a kindergarten Sunday school class? Why?

2. If you met a teacher who feels that games have no part in a Bible teaching program, how could you justify games to this person?

Study Projects

1. Choose a Bible story and invent some story-related movements to do in a lesson with it.

2. Examine kindergarten lessons from two or more publishers, and evaluate them on their use of movement and games.

3. Choose one of the games in this chapter or another kindergarten level game you know and write a

paragraph or two telling how you can justify it from an educational standpoint. Tell both how it fits the child's developmental level and what he can gain from it cognitively, physically, and socio-emotionally.

Mini-Teaching and Observation Experience

Work with a partner on this. Each of you prepare a game of a different type. For instance, one of you can prepare a language-ritual game and one can prepare a game with cards, such as Concentration. Or use a singing game idea from Chapter 6. While one partner leads a game, the other observes, then exchange places for the second game.

Observation tasks. Do the children listen attentively to pre-game instructions? Do they seem to retain this information throughout the game, or do they need more instruction as they proceed? Do some children catch on more quickly than others? What differences do you notice among the children? Can you "see" any thinking going on as the game proceeds? Can you see improvement and learning of any kind? What?

Evaluation. Do your observation notes suggest to you any way the games might be modified to obtain fuller participation or higher interest? How? Do they suggest any better way for the teacher to get things started quickly, or keep the interest high? How?

CHAPTER 8: CLASSROOM AND LESSON MATERIALS

Questions

1. How much of a Sunday school hour do you think should be used for group, teacher-led learning? How much for individual learning at centers? Why? Do you think most other teachers should do it this way too?

2. What is your opinion of block areas for Sunday school use? Home-play areas? Nature centers? Book

centers?

Study Projects
1. Plan, gather materials, and set up a needed center in a kindergarten room in your church.

2. Inspect the kindergarten room or rooms in your church, with a team if possible, and plan how they might be improved. Write a list of things that might be done and try to justify each suggested change. Why is it needed? How will it be better than now?

3. Draw what you consider an ideal room plan, and list the equipment needed for it.

Classroom Observation
Arrange a visit in a church that uses a variety of learning centers. Briefly look at each, then choose one to settle down in and watch the action. How much learning do you think happens here? What learning?

Maxi-Teaching Experience
Using a published lesson, prepare and teach a full Sunday school lesson for a kindergarten group.

Index

Abraham, singing game, 122
Abstractions, 21, 29, 30, 42, 49, 53
Action Review, game, 153
Action rhymes, 132-134
Aesthetic growth, 103, 106
All Night, All Day, song, 115
Angel concept, 45, 52, 80

Bettelheim, Bruno, 34, 48
Block center, 7, 11
Book center, 7
Brain, 45

Chalk drawings, 59-62
Choral speaking, 134-136
Clapping stories, 136-138
Competition, 147, 153
Concentration, game, 151
Concrete operational stage, 17, 46
Concreteness, 21, 27, 29, 30, 32, 42, 49, 52, 53
Cooperation, 22, 125, 141, 145, 149, 153
Cratty, Bryant J., 143
Creativity, 97-101, 125
Curriculum materials, 172-176

Death concept, 28, 41-43
Delacato, Carl H., 142
Discipline, 74-75
Doman, Glenn J., 142
Drawing Review, game, 154
Drawings as visuals, 59-62

Eareckson, Joni, 98, 105
Egocentricity, 15-16
Elijah Went Up, rhyme, 134
Emotional growth, 13, 21-25, 96

Fear, 22
Fels Research Institute, 45
Fisherman Tag, game 148
Flannelgraph, 55, 77-84
Forgiveness concept, 53, 56
Frye, Northrup, 51

Getman, R., 142
Giving, clapping story, 136
God concept, 27, 28
God Gave Adam Work to Do, singing game, 122
God's Temple, song, 119
God Made the Bear, singing game, 123

Heart concept, 45, 46
Heart research, 45, 46
Heaven concept, 42, 45, 80
Heaven is a Happy Place, singing game, 123
Hell concept, 42, 45
Holy Spirit concept, 29
Horse and Chariot, game, 148
Human meaning, 19, 37, 38, 50
Humphrey, James, 143
Hymns for children, 113, 114

I Am Bound for the Promised Land, song 113
I Will Love the Bible, song, 118
Images, mental, 70, 72

Jesus concept, 27, 28
Jesus Made People Well, clapping story, 137
Joshua and the Soldiers, game, 145
Just a Little Oil, rhyme, 133
Just As I Am, song, 114

Kephart, Newell C., 142
Kinesthetic learning, 143ff
King concept, 52
Kohlberg, Lawrence, 33
Lacey, John and Beatrice, 45
Language, 15, 22-23, 39-40, 52, 53, 145
Learning centers, 160-168
Listen and Clap, game 155

Manipulative stage, 85-87, 94
May I—Thank You, game, 148

Memory, 132, 138-139
Mental characteristics, 12, 13, 15-21
Methods of teaching, 71
Moral learning, 31-34, 48
Mosston, Muska, 143
Motor learning, 142ff

Number concepts, 18, 19, 142

Obedience, 53, 101, 102
Oh, How I Love Jesus, song, 109

Participation stories, 62-67
Physical characteristics, 14, 15
Piaget, Jean, 15-17, 41, 142
Picture Books, 54-55, 71-75
Planning skill in children, 21, 22
Play equipment, 171
Poor Donkey, game, 152
Preoperational stage, 15, 46
Psychology of Teaching Methods, The, 71
Punishment-reward, 33
Puppets, 55-59

Questioning, 53 54

Rachel and Jacob, singing game, 124
Racial differences, 24, 25
Representative stage, 88-95, 102
Reward-punishment, 33
Rhythm, 126, 132, 138-139
Rhythm instruments, 11, 65-67, 125-131
Room at the Inn, game, 145
Room equipment, 170
Room size, 169
Running to the Ark, game, 144

Salvation, 34-40
Sea of Galilee, song, 117
Self-concept, 43-45, 141
Self-confidence, 14, 43-45, 141
Sentence Game, 148, 149
Sex differences, 22-24
Shepherd Tag, game, 151
Sin concept, 33, 53
Singing range, 108

Singing voice, 108
Social growth, 21-25, 96, 141
Sound stories, 65-67
Space concepts, 19-21, 60, 80
Stick Man Review, game, 154
Symbols, 29, 88-94, 99

Tax Money, game, 146
Tents for Sale, game 146
The Lepers, rhyme, 133
Time concepts, 19, 80
Trinity concept, 30, 31
Twinkle, Twinkle Little Star, song, 114

Visuals, 54, 55, 76-80

What is Missing?, game, 148
Who Built the Ark?, song, 116
Whole method, 109, 110
Words, use of, 15, 39, 52, 69, 76, 155